AUTISM
and Independence

**Assessments and Interventions
to Prepare Teens for Adult Life**

Daniel Marston, PhD, ABPP

Published by
PESI Publishing & Media
PESI, Inc.
3839 White Ave
Eau Claire, WI 54703

Cover: Amy Rubenzer
Editing: Teresa Garland
Layout: Bookmasters & Amy Rubenzer

ISBN: 9781683731955

PESI
Publishing
& Media
www.publishing.pesi.com

About the Author

Daniel Marston, PhD, ABPP is a licensed psychologist with over 20 years of experience working with individuals with autism and other neurodevelopmental conditions. He is the owner and chief psychologist at Marston Psychological Services near Pittsburgh, PA. Dr. Marston is board-certified in Behavioral & Cognitive Psychology by the American Board of Professional Psychology (ABPP). He has written a book, book chapters and several professional papers on the application of scientific research to clinical work.

Table of Contents

Introduction

If you are someone who recognizes and appreciates how complex the lives of people with autism can be, then this book is for you. I wrote this to help you help others who have to deal daily with the struggles autism presents. I wrote this to help you help them handle social barriers of autism made worse by the social mess that is adolescence. I wrote this to help you help them with problems while not taking away anything that makes someone with autism stand out.

And I wrote this to explain the complexities of autism AND the research behind why any of this stuff works. Because if there is no research to our work, then what are we doing? Trust me, I know that research isn't the whole story. And much of it seems done by people who spend so much time in a lab or looking at statistics that they forgot what real life is like. But it is a starting point. And it does show that we're not all out there just making this up as we go along.

I have worked for over 20 years with teenagers and young adults with autism. I have seen interventions work very, very well and interventions work very, very poorly. I have seen the deep sadness that occurs when someone is excluded for reasons they do not understand. And I have seen the triumphs when teenage clients say "F-You" to society's expectations and live life the way they want. I have also seen parents insist loudly their child needs "more friends!!" while that same child (now a young adult) yells back "no, I don't!!" There is no easy pattern to any of this. But I will share with you how to make it work.

chapter 1

Autism and the Teenage/Young Adult Years

Alright, let's review some basics here. You need four things for a diagnosis of autism:

1. Communication problems
2. Social difficulties
3. Repetitive behaviors
4. Neurological cause

That's it. If you don't have all four, then you don't have autism. You might have something else, but it isn't autism.

You might have Social Communication Disorder. That's a new diagnosis used when you have communication and social problems but not the repetitive behaviors. If you work with anybody who was diagnosed several years ago, you might have seen this diagnosed as Pervasive Developmental Disorder.

Or you might have Reactive Attachment Disorder. That's when you have the three symptoms but not the neurological cause. The cause here is typically emotional trauma at a young age (the "attachment" part is emotional attachment). I often call this "autism with psychological causes."

Both of these other diagnoses might respond to approaches that help someone with autism. But they are different from autism and someone with either of those diagnoses does not have autism.

One other thing all types of autism have in common is that they are NOT treated with medication. Some of the symptoms might be helped with meds. Risperdal, for example, is often used to treat aggressiveness in autism. But you do not treat autism with medication.

Trust me, the pharmaceutical industry would LOVE (I mean LOVE, LOVE, LOVE) to advertise "The Ultimate Treatment" for autism. But they can't. Because they don't have it. For right now, behavioral and psychological interventions are what you need to treat autism. Everything else is just filler.

Defining autism is straightforward. What makes it complex is presentation and cause. Presentation because every person who has autism presents differently. You may only have three main symptoms, but they can present in millions of different ways.

Symptom severity and intellectual functioning are two major examples of things impacting noticeably on the way autism presents. Autistic symptoms run the gamut from minimal impact to severe impact. Individuals with autism run the gamut from severely intellectually impaired to intellectually gifted.

Intellectual disabilities make life more difficult for people with autism. Teenagers and young adults with intellectual disabilities are typically lonelier than other people. They report fewer friends and poorer quality of friendships than typically-developed teenagers. They also report fewer social activities with their peers (Taheri, Perry & Minnes, 2016).

Cause is the other factor impacting on autism's complexity. All causes of autism are neurological. But neurological causes are wide and varied. Over 10 years ago, there were at least 60 diseases thought to be associated with autism (Coleman, 2005). Rapid advances in neurological technologies since then has increased considerably the number of possible neurological causes. Some recent diseases associated with autism identified in recent years include a genetic disorder called "22q13 deletion syndrome" (Yitzchak, Jamison, Tavassoli & Kolevzon, 2017), epilepsy (Keller, Basta, Salerno & Elia, 2017), brain carnitine deficiency and congenital cytomegalovirus infection (Garofoli et al. 2017).

Two brain areas typically associated with autism are the amygdala and the hippocampus. They are impacted differently by the different neurological causes, but they tend to be involved in most cases. These are areas of the brain associated with emotion perception and regulation, and that is thought to have some significance in behaviors associated with autism.

Children with autism tend to have a larger amygdala and hippocampus than children without autism. This difference continues in the teenage years (Groen, Teluij, Buitelaar & Tendolkar, 2010).

These neurological causes impact an individual throughout his or her life. They impact each stage of development differently throughout a person's life. When it comes to the teenage years, that impact is particularly direct. Here's why:

Autism is a condition impacting social connections. And, to teenagers, the rank order of important things is as follows:

1. Social connections
2. Everything else

So, the most important thing to teenagers is one thing significantly impacted by autism. When someone with autism hits the teenage years, they are often heading towards a time when what matters most to people their age is something they are often the worst at (or at least the least comfortable). Because of all this, transitioning from adolescence, and then to young adulthood, is a vulnerable time for individuals with autism (O'Hearn et al. 2014).

Every teenager or young adult with autism with whom I have worked presented with difficulties related to socialization. Depression due to loneliness, anger due to being bullied, or anxiety due to pressure put on them by parents or siblings to "make some friends" are common complaints.

What is particularly sad in many of these cases is that it is not the client who thought their behaviors were a problem. They may have been comfortable with their social behaviors or even with their lack of friends. I have even been very impressed by the ability of some clients with autism to be very content being by themselves and doing things alone (wishing sometimes I had more of that ability myself!).

But these were individuals who wanted to fit in. They wanted to feel, as we all do, that they were making progress towards being independent. They wanted to see themselves as being on the right track towards doing what they need to do in order to be adult-like.

However, other people were showing that this was not happening. They were making fun of them, criticizing their lack of social connections, brushing off their attempts to get employed, or just ignoring them. And it was then that they decided things weren't going well and they needed to change something.

What I learned over the years is that a therapist's or counselor's first job when working with a teenager or young adult with autism is helping them target what actually needs changing. It may be behaviors—social behaviors, communication behaviors and anger management behaviors are common targets. But it also might be negative thinking. Particularly negative thinking about themselves. Feeling bad about themselves because others treat them badly is common. Deciding that they are not meeting society's expectations for how a person should be or act is also common.

Some other psychological issues you want to look for when working with a teenager or young adult with autism:

1. Social withdrawal, irritability and hyperactivity are three behavioral symptoms associated with autism that tend to change during the teenage years. Social withdrawal tends to get worse during teenage years while hyperactivity and irritability tend to improve as individuals with autism get older (Anderson, Maye & Lord, 2011).

2. Repetitive behaviors tend to show the least improvement on their own as children with autism get older (Chowdhury, Benson & Hillier, 2010). These often need to be addressed in counseling or therapy because of how often they impact on social interactions.

3. Daily living skills become more important as individuals get older, and problems there might impact a young adult with autism working towards independence. Individuals with autism tend to show improvement in daily living skills during early adolescence and up until their early 20s. These improvements level off in their late 20s and are much less noticeable when an intellectual disability is present (Smith, Maenner & Seltzer, 2012).

4. As children with autism get older they show more executive functioning problems. They have more problems with what is called metacognitive abilities compared to younger children (Rosenthal et al. 2013). This is often called ability to think about thinking. Planning ability, problem-solving strategies, self-monitoring of behaviors and self-correction of errors are four examples of specific abilities considered to be metacognitive abilities. These are all problems that may need to be addressed in therapy because of how much they can impact on a teenager or young adult with autism trying to do more things on his or her own.

5. Dealing with cognitive difficulties is a topic that may need to be addressed in therapy. Cognitive difficulties might impact on how much progress a person feels she or he is making towards independence, but

there is not much evidence that the difficulties themselves become worse as individuals with autism enter adolescence and young adulthood. A review of 25 studies showed that cognitive ability, language skills and social functioning actually remained relatively stable for individuals with autism throughout their childhood and teenage years (Magiati, Tay & Howlin, 2014).

6. Differences in behavioral patterns for teenagers and young adults with autism were also reflected in parental rating scales. Parents rated teenagers with autism lower than teenagers without autism in terms of psychological well-being, physical well-being and social support with peers. Involvement in community activities was one factor that tended to improve functioning in all of these areas (Biggs & Carter, 2016). Parents' reports showed improvements in terms of social interactions, repetitive/stereotyped behaviors, adaptive behaviors, and emotional responsiveness to other people for adolescents with autism compared to their ratings as children.

7. Adolescents with high-functioning autism showed more improvements in their areas compared to low-functioning autism. Also, the degree to which the children and adolescents were engaged with peers tended to predict improvements in adaptive living skills in adolescence. This was the case even for children and adolescents with autism who had intellectual disabilities (McGovern & Sigman, 2005).

Following is a case example of a teenager with autism. This case does not include interventions, but talks about the reasons Sarah presented to therapy. I included it here to provide an illustration of the emotional challenges often faced by teenagers with autism.

Case Study
Teen with Autism Depression

Sarah is a teenage girl who presents to therapy with depression. She has autism and was first diagnosed with autism when she was a very young child. She received behavior therapy throughout her childhood and even made some friends at school. She was generally happy in elementary school and middle school.

But then things changed when she got to high school. During therapy she talked about how her behaviors and interests stayed pretty much the same when she got to high school compared to when she was in elementary and middle school. But kids reacted differently to her. When she wanted to talk at length about cartoons, her peers did not let her talk or show any interest.

In earlier years, her peers had at least let her be around them while she talked, even if they were doing something else. But this was not happening anymore. High school students were making fun of her, laughing at her or just walking away when she talked. She was lonely and did not really understand why. She was only talking about what interested her and was not being mean to other kids.

Why were they being so mean to her? She hadn't changed her behaviors at all and was just acting in ways that made her comfortable. Clearly this wasn't good enough for the rest of the world.

Sarah decided that she wanted to kill herself. She told her parents and they determined or realized she was serious. They took her to a hospital to be evaluated. She was very open and specific with the therapist who evaluated her. She wanted to die because she just didn't fit in and the rest of the world was so mean to her. She told the therapist that she would take 42 aspirins and drink a bottle of drain cleaner. It was this specificity that really caused the therapist concern.

Sarah had always been very detailed-oriented and was being no different now. She had also been serious that the world needed to be fair and she was not seeing anything fair now about how other people treated her. She was admitted to the hospital and stayed for two weeks.

Sarah entered outpatient therapy after her hospital discharge. She was no longer actively suicidal, but continued to repeat feeling very sad about her life. She was lonely and was not making any friends. She actually was not unhappy about doing things by herself, she enjoyed being by herself, but was unhappy because so many people expected her to have friends. Her parents and other family members often asked her repeatedly "Why don't you have any friends that you could spend time with?" and she was getting tired of it.

It was also distressing for her that other kids not only did not like being around her, but were very obvious and mean about it. They would not just do what they wanted when she was around, but would purposely walk away from her when she talked. They made comments about her speaking loud enough for her to hear. They were negative about her and were making sure that she knew it.

She loved a television show about a group of high school friends and would often talk about that show. But now other kids around her mocked her and made negative comments about the characters. Even her favorite TV show was no longer a refuge. She hated her life and really, really did not know why.

Sarah had autistic symptoms that did not change much as she got older. She also had interests that did not change much as she got older. But as she got older, they elicited much more negative reactions from her peers. Sarah was also relatively happy with her interests and behaviors, but was not happy with how other people responded to them. Others were telling her that what she was doing was wrong and that was causing her distress.

It was not her autistic symptoms causing her difficulties but, rather, the response she received from others. Sarah wanted social connectedness but could not find it. And, finally, take note of the despair. She not only has intense difficulties, but does not know how they got there. Her depression is associated with strong feelings of hopelessness and helplessness.

chapter 2
Clinical Assessment

Clients don't initially give me much information that is useful for guiding treatment. When we first talk, the client (or his parents) will say that he has autism, or that he thinks he has it. He may provide information about past treatments, problems related to autism (or that lead them to suspect autism) and other behavioral or emotional difficulties. But that is usually it. They provide me this information and then look to me to decide what comes next. Here are two common scenarios:

Case Study
Teen with Autism

Janet was 15 years old when she and her parents came to see me. She had been diagnosed with autism by her school at six years of age using formal testing and began receiving autistic support services that year. Janet's parents are concerned about her and about how depressed she seems. She has no friends and spends all her time alone.

They gave me a copy of her school's initial evaluation report as well as a copy of the most recent psychological evaluation report from her high school. Her parents have read the reports several times but admit they do not understand much of what is in the reports because they are filled with technical jargon.

Janet had services provided in her home when she was young and her parents described those services as helpful for addressing her social skills. She made some friends during elementary and middle school, but seemed to lose contact with those friends when she started high school. She has seemed more withdrawn and depressed since she started high school. Her parents reported that this seemed to coincide with when she stopped having contact with her previous friends, but they were not certain what might have led to this change. When I talked to Janet about this, she did not disagree with what her parents had related about her background or about her depression. But when I questioned her about the cause of her increased depression she stated only, "I don't know."

Case Study
Non-Diagnosed Young Adult

Jack is a young adult who has not had a formal diagnosis of autism. He recently started a job, his first full-time job, at a local home improvement mega-store. He had held other part-time jobs before, but had problems getting along with his co-workers. He is now having frequent run-ins with co-workers at his new job. He has gotten into loud arguments with other employees when they were not doing things exactly the ways that he thought they should.

He recently got written up by his supervisor because he made a threat of violence against another employee with whom he was having a disagreement. He stated that the other employee made fun of him when he was getting angry because the other employee was not loading things onto a car the way Jack thought that he should. He got very focused on this issue and spent at least 15 minutes yelling at the other employee "because he was doing it wrong."

Jack's history of arguing with others goes back to school, where he received support services to decrease argumentative behaviors with students and teachers. He went to a small school that did not have autistic support services and it was not clear whether the school staff would have pursued those services if they were available.

As a teenager, Jack was in therapy twice, and both therapists told him they thought he had autism. Jack stated that he disagreed with what his therapists told him, including that he had autism, and this was what led him to leave therapy both times. He said that now he is thinking that those therapists may have been correct and that he is now trying to figure out what to do in order to keep from losing his job. Jack did not have any additional information from any healthcare professionals or school staff who had worked with him previously.

Notice that with each of these scenarios the background and clinical information is very limited. And that is to be expected. It is not really the job of new clients to tell me what might be contributing to the problems. It is my job, as a clinician, to use my clinical knowledge, experience and skills to try and figure out what is contributing to the problems and develop a course of treatment. I certainly look to clients to tell me what they can, but the bulk of this responsibility falls on me. I turn to a formal clinical assessment to get this process started.

Clinical assessments are essential but can also be time-consuming. Individuals come into therapy because they need help. But when too much time is spent assessing problems they can become uncomfortable and angry.

Clinical assessments using formal psychological tests can also be very expensive. Assessment instruments cost money, sometimes a lot of money, and the costs can rack up pretty quickly.

Every clinical professional wants to do a thorough job for their clients, but if assessments take so long that the clients get angry, that hurts the client. And if the assessment materials cost so much the professional essentially works for free, then that hurts the professional—which, in turns, hurts the client.

In my experience, many therapists and counselors equate psychological assessment with just "psychological testing." I think testing can be important but it also may be unnecessary. You may be able to gather information from previous assessments and eliminate the need for testing.

IQ testing is a good example of this type of testing. These days, most teenagers and young adults receive some sort of IQ testing during their school years. This is especially true of teenagers and young adults with autism. If they had shown any signs of behavioral difficulties during the earlier school years it is very likely the school would have referred them for some sort of educational testing. That would likely involve some sort of IQ testing. Since IQ scores do not vary much throughout a person's life, barring any sort of brain injury, you really do not need to do an IQ test again.

Now, don't get me wrong. I am not opposed to formal psychological testing. I do recognize that testing is essential if information is not otherwise available. Like all psychologists, I have certain tests that I use at specific times for specific purposes. But I think alternatives to testing are important for your client's time and resources.

I utilize an assessment approach that focuses on clinical interviews and reviews of clinical and educational records before considering any testing. Psychological tests can enter into the assessment picture, but only after making sure that all previous materials have been sufficiently considered.

My approach to autism assessment for teenagers and young adults asks the following set of seven questions. They are modified from an article on autism (Huerta & Lord, 2012) to particularly focus on teenagers and young adults:

1. What diagnostic classification best describes this person's pattern of behaviors and difficulties? If no diagnosis is confirmed, how often should they continue to be monitored?
2. What is this individual's overall level of functioning? Is cognitive functioning, language ability, or learning impaired? Or are results suspect?
3. Are there additional behaviors and/or diagnoses to consider for this person when planning treatment?
4. What behaviors/symptoms are most concerning to the individual and/or family/caregivers? What role would they like to play in the client's treatment?
5. Given the current constellation of symptoms, what are the most important targets for intervention at this time?
6. Given family circumstances, community resources, and other contextual factors, what recommendations are most appropriate?
7. What is the prognosis for this client in the short term? Is there enough information to make predictions about prognosis over the long term?

#1: What is the Diagnostic Picture?

Specifically, the question here is does this person have autism? This is an important question for two reasons. First, just because someone says they have autism doesn't mean that they do. Second, autism tends to respond to some very specific interventions. If someone does not have autism, then your treatment plan might look completely different than if they do.

I typically ask a new client who presents with possible autism what makes her say she has autism (or thinks she has autism). If she says she has already been diagnosed, then I find out where (or ask her parents or other family members where). Many teenagers and young adults with autism have been evaluated previously at school or treatment centers. If I can get those records, then I am off to a pretty good start. It is not necessarily the case that I will agree with what previous evaluations showed, but this will often provide some pretty strong evidence.

As complex as autism can be, it has only three main symptoms. If you look at the *DSM-5®* (American Psychiatric Association Publications, 2013), the main diagnostic guide for mental health professionals, you will see a lengthy description under the heading "Autism Spectrum Disorders." But when you get through that description you see the three main symptoms of autism:

1. Social difficulties
2. Poor communication skills
3. Perseveration and/or stereotypical behaviors

So, whether you are using formal testing, a screening instrument or a clinical interview, you are looking to see if all three of these symptoms are present. If only one or two are present, then it is not autism. If you have evidence that all three are clearly present, then you likely are looking at autism.

These are repetitive behaviors that impact on the individual's functioning. If this type of symptom is not present, but the other two are, you are not dealing with autism, but this may instead be a Social Communication Disorder. This is also the symptom that is most likely to come up for individuals who were diagnosed with an autistic-type disorder when younger but who would not qualify for that diagnosis now.

In previous editions of the *DSM* there was a diagnostic category called Pervasive Developmental Disorder Not Otherwise Specified (or PDD NOS) that fit many individuals with social and communication problems but not perseveration or stereotyped behaviors. That was considered a type of autism whereas the newer Social Communication Disorder is not.

Before moving on, let me address briefly what I would do if I did evaluate a teenager or young adult and decided they had Social Communication Disorder. In most cases, I would treat him or her using the interventions throughout this book for social and communication problems.

Perseveration is not a symptom of this disorder so interventions for that would not be relevant. But I have found that the same types of communication and social skills interventions for someone with autism do work for someone with Social Communication Disorder. You just need to keep in mind that, at least at the time I write this book, the research has not yet caught up to specifically address this issue.

During the first visit with a new client, I always provide a clinical interview for clients and determine afterwards if additional screening or testing is needed. When evaluating a teenager or young adult who might have autism, I gear that interview towards the three main autistic symptoms. I ask about any history of the symptoms and ask whether they observed the symptoms and if others reported that they observed the symptoms. I will also do my own observations of the individual during the interview.

A clinical interview is an interpersonal situation and, as such, allows me a good opportunity to see if I see any of the symptoms the individual reports, and if so, how much those symptoms impact their interpersonal functioning.

Here are specific questions relevant to an autism diagnosis that are important in a clinical interview:

- Does he make eye contact and maintain eye contact when speaking with you?
- Does she seem to understand basic social behaviors when interacting with you?
- Does he seem to stay focused on certain topics for a few minutes at a time?
- Does she continue to stay focused on those topics even when other topics are brought up?
- Is it difficult to redirect him away from topics on which he is focused?
- Does she report having any friends or having any sort of social network?

- Do family members report that social relationships have been difficult for him?
- Is there any evidence of self-stimulatory behaviors during the interview?
- Does she or her family members report that self-stimulatory behaviors can be very disruptive throughout every day?
- Do you observe or hear about him having problems with being empathic (or putting himself in someone else's shoes)?

Notice how each of these questions relate directly to one of the three main symptom categories for autism.

I often find the clinical interview is sufficient for allowing me a definite opinion about whether or not my client has autism. This is especially true if I have school records or past treatment records, or even just reports from previous teachers or treatment professionals, that support an autism diagnosis.

But sometimes the interview and records review are not sufficient. This may be because past records are nonexistent or inconclusive (e.g., one treatment professional gives an autism diagnosis while the other does not). Or it may be that the client's presentation during assessment is not consistent with autism. In these cases psychological testing in some form is needed. This may include longer psychological tests or shorter psychological screening instruments.

Autism tests involve the most commitment in terms of time and expense. They also provide the most information and the most definitive diagnoses. The most comprehensive psychological test for autism is the Autism Diagnostic Observation Schedule, 2nd edition (ADOS-2; Lord et al. 2012). It is very comprehensive but also has several disadvantages. For one thing, it is very lengthy. It also can only be conducted by someone who has been formally trained on the instrument. It can be used for teenagers and young adults but can take several hours to complete. And probably the most prohibitive aspect of the test is the cost as, at the time this book was written, it costs almost $2,000.

Another psychological test for autism, applicable for both teenager and young adult clients, is the Autism Diagnostic Interview, Revised (ADI-R; Rutter, LeCouteur & Lord, 2003). It is a comprehensive and very structured interview method that addresses all major areas of autism. It is not particularly expensive (about $400 at the time this book was written) but is very time-consuming. This instrument can take from 1½-2 hours to administer and requires completion of a formal training course before administering the instrument.

Screening instruments are often more frequently part of clinical autism assessment, given that they are shorter and less demanding. One screening instrument that is similar to the ADI-R, but only takes 10 minutes or so to complete, is the Social Communication Questionnaire (SCQ; Rutter, Bailey & Lord, 2003). As a screening instrument, it is most often used to indicate whether a more comprehensive evaluation (like those involving the ADOS-2 or ADI-R) is needed. One potentially very useful aspect of this instrument is that it is published in at least 16 different languages (including Danish, Romanian, Icelandic and Spanish).

Another screening instrument for autism designed specifically for teenagers and young adults with intellectual disabilities is the Diagnostic Behavioral Assessment for ASD – Revised (DiBAS-R; Sappock et al. 2014). This is an instrument based on criteria set in the *DSM-5* and ICD-10 and is based on caregivers completing 19 Likert-scaled items. It is designed specifically for completion by caregivers who may or may not have any understanding of autism. This means that the items are written in such a way that someone who does not know what sort of language and descriptions are used with autism could easily complete them.

#2: What is the Individual's Overall Level of Functioning?

Most teenagers and young adults I see have previously received some sort of formal testing through their schools or treatment professionals. Individuals who have, or might have, autism typically have long-standing problems with communication and social skills that schools and parents have tried to address. Previous attempts to answer the question "Why do they act this way?" usually result in IQ testing and other types of cognitive tests.

What I do is gather together as much of the material I can that tells me something about the person's functional abilities. I will obtain IQ scores if they are available and will get school records to see how the person performed academically. I can also gauge the person's use of language in the clinical interview and obtain information from the person and their family about adaptive functioning. This means that I can often answer this second question by gathering records and information in the clinical interview.

When considering formal IQ tests, the two main ones are the Wechsler Adult Intelligence Scale (WAIS-IV; Wechsler, 2004) and then the Stanford-Binet (Thorndike, 1986). Both are widely used and widely accepted. The WAIS-IV is the most common and probably the one most people are referring to when they use the term IQ.

One possible benefit to the Stanford-Binet is that it can be used for children and adults. In contrast, the age range for the WAIS-IV starts at age 16. There is a children's version of the Wechsler that you need to use for individuals under 16. So, if you are working with children as well as teenagers and adults in your practice, you might want to consider the Stanford-Binet. It is nearly as well-accepted as the Wechsler and can save you from having to buy an additional test.

There is no doubt that intellectual ability is the most important cognitive area to consider. It covers a large range of different abilities and gives you a strong idea of how well the person is going to understand, recall and use the interventions you provide. Another area of cognitive functioning that is important to consider is executive functioning. This is the area that addresses how well the person is able to focus on what you are telling them, make some sense of the information, and focus enough (without being distracted) on actually making use of what you present.

Executive functioning involves four main areas: working memory, attention, cognitive flexibility and inhibitory control. Here are some of the questions I ask during the clinical interview to address these areas:

- Does the individual show problems with taking in new information and then using it later?
- Can the individual think about situations in more than one way?
- Are ignoring distractions and/or waiting to respond clear problems for this individual?

A more formal and comprehensive measure of executive functioning, that is not too long or cumbersome, is the Brief Rating Inventory of Executive Functioning (BRIEF; Roth & Gioia, 2005). This is a scale specifically for older teenagers and young adults. What is particularly useful about it is that it measures executive functioning specifically through the use of behavioral observations. You can perform a complete assessment based on information and observations you obtain during a clinical interview and do not have to necessarily have the person complete special tasks as part of the assessment. The BRIEF gives a good indication of how likely it is that executive functioning problems are going to interfere with the person's ability to learn and use new material, and also deal with problematic and emotionally upsetting situations.

Expressive language ability is, along with IQ, a very good predictor of long-term treatment outcome, so it is an especially important characteristic to measure. Expressive language instruments address not only how well someone communicates but also identify what approaches help her or him communicate most effectively. This is all useful information for deciding how best to help your clients get their feelings and thoughts across during sessions. The most comprehensive measure of language ability for teenagers and young adults is the Test of Adolescent and Adult Language, Fourth Edition (Hamill, Brown, Larsen & Wiederholt, 2016).

Adaptive functioning is the fourth major area to consider as part of this assessment question. This refers to how well the person handles new situations and deals with problems. Impaired adaptive functioning is one criterion needed for an intellectual disability diagnosis and often plays a major role in how well an individual with both autism and intellectual disability deals with difficulties. Luiselli et al. (2001) found that the most common adaptive measure used with individuals suspected of having an autism diagnosis is the Vineland Adaptive Behavior Scales (Balla, & Cicchetti, 1984).

This instrument assesses the person's ability to effectively handle communication, daily living skills and socialization. It is based on information collected from clinical interviews, parental/caregiver reports and behavioral observations. There are also supplementary norms available specifically for individuals with autism (Carter et al. 1998).

#3: Are There Additional Diagnoses to Consider?

ADHD is also a diagnosis commonly associated with autism. Recent estimates have put the rate at which ADHD and autism occur together (called "comorbid ADHD/ASD") at 22% (Manohar et al. 2018). Attention problems are not specifically a symptom of autism but may be a problem alongside autism. These often make autistic symptoms worse and add to the degree of effort needed to get the teenager or young adult to focus on what you try to address.

One formal assessment measure that is very useful for assessing ADHD, and can be used with children, teenagers and adults, is the Brown ADHD Scales (Brown, 2009).

Conducting an assessment of sensory problems is also beneficial when trying to determine if ADHD is present with *or* in autism. This is because sensory deficits, along with a tendency to react very strongly and loudly when problems occur, is often present in autism. When strong reactions to sensory problems occur, they can often look like hyperactivity and other symptoms of ADHD (Schaaf & Lane, 2015). One of the best instruments for conducting a sensory problems assessment in teenagers and adults with autism is the Adult/Adolescent Sensory Profile (Brown & Dunn, 2002).

Mood and anxiety disorders are also common disorders that co-exist alongside autism. Teenagers and young adults with autism often experience emotional difficulties and anxiety because of the problems they face. Loneliness, worry about social situations, academic difficulties, teasing and bullying are just some of the issues that can contribute to emotional and anxiety difficulties in teenagers and young adults with autism.

Two scales that would be useful for measuring depression and anxiety in teenagers and young adults with autism, are the Beck Depressive Inventory-II (Beck, Steer & Brown, 1996) and the Beck Anxiety Inventory (Beck & Steer, 1990). Another test specifically used for measuring anxiety for adolescents with autism is the Developmental Disability–Child Global Assessment Scale (White, Smith & Schry, 2014).

#4: What Behaviors and Symptoms are Most Concerning to the Individual and/or Family Members?

This is the area I find that individuals coming into therapy are most ready to discuss. They may not know much in terms of specifics regarding past treatments and diagnoses, but they know what is bothering them now. I carefully take note of the family members' concerns versus the individual client's concerns and then try to ascertain how much weight to give to each. I find this to be an area of difficulty, but one that gets resolved with time.

Individuals with autism often have relied a good deal on family members throughout their lives and may still be expecting their family members are going to do most of the talking for them. I often even find that teenage and young adult clients with autism do not want to provide information and are eager for their family members to provide the bulk of information I need.

During the assessment phase, I think the best approach to take is to just get information from whoever is willing to give information and whoever the client is willing to let give information. Sorting out whose concerns and opinions should be emphasized can be done later. At the very beginning I collect information from everyone involved and particularly look for patterns of concerns. If there are multiple people reporting that the client has problems in a certain area, then that does give some weight on needing to focus on that problem.

I try to keep the assessment phase one where all individuals involved with the client can express their concerns about what needs to be addressed. My view is that addressing how much the client does or does not want others involved with their treatment can wait to later. But it is not always possible to do this if you are dealing with a client over 18 years of age. Because the truth of the matter is that if an individual is over 18 years old, and has not legally been determined to be unable to make independent decisions, then she or he is not required to have anyone else involved in their assessment or treatment.

If an adult client says they do not want parents or caregivers involved, then there is nothing I or anyone else can do about it except to respect their wishes. I can review with the client what this means and make sure he or she knows that if they say I cannot talk with their parents then I just cannot talk to them. This can be a difficult conversation, and one that I prefer to keep for after therapy starts, but sometimes it just cannot be avoided during assessment.

#5: What are the Most Important Targets for Treatment?

This is an offshoot of the discussions with clients and family members. Here the focus is on identifying the specific areas of concerns that each bring up. Some of the specific questions that help focus clients and family members on material needed for answering this question include:

- What behavior problems have caused the most difficulties over the past four weeks?
- How many days per week are the person's behavior problems causing noticeable difficulties?

- On a scale of 0 to 10, what is the average severity of the person's behavior problems in an average week?
- Please list four of the most recent episodes that you can remember where this person's behavior problems caused difficulties for themselves and/or other people?
- In an average week, how many episodes are there where the person's behaviors cause noticeable difficulties for themselves and/or other people?
- In an average week, what are the most common types of difficulties that the person's behaviors cause for themselves and/or other people?

As I stated earlier, I often look for patterns in problems that are reported by clients and family members. If more than one person reports a problem this often, but not always, gives it some weight. But if a family member or teacher is reporting a problem but the client is not, I do think this is worthy of further discussion. But I would be interested in knowing why others are seeing a problem that the client does not.

One example of how to approach this with a client is by using this script:

> *I notice that in my review of your records and talking with your teacher, that your teacher mentioned several times that you had problems getting angry with other people. I also noted that you and your parents both mentioned that you had difficulties when other people did not act exactly the way you thought they should and that you often started yelling in those situations. It was also not my impression that you disagreed with what your parents said but you didn't specifically mention having problems with anger. So, I wonder if you think we need to include anger as a problem that we address here?*

#6: What Community Resources and Recommendations are Most Important?

I try to keep track of all the resources available in my area and my clients' areas that are specifically designed to help individuals with autism. If I am not familiar with the area where a new client lives, I check online before or just after an assessment so I can provide information about resources they might find helpful. Some specific types of resources that I think are important to include in this search are:

- Autism support organizations
- Schools for students with special needs
- Social skills groups
- Treatment centers specializing in autism

#7: What are the Short-Term and Long-Term Prognoses?

This is a question that speaks directly to motivation and symptom severity. My clinical judgment usually gives me a good sense of how motivated the client is to work in therapy. Symptom severity is usually reflected in past treatment and assessment records. I can also get a good sense of symptom severity in how the person presents during the clinical interview.

One formal psychological assessment instrument that is designed specifically for measuring symptom severity is the Autism Spectrum Quotient. There is a version for adolescents (Baron-Cohen et al. 2006) and one for adults (Baron-Cohen et al. 2001). Both of these give a score reflecting severity of autistic traits and the degree to which those traits are likely to impact on an individual's functioning.

Comprehensive Assessments

I outlined throughout this chapter the approaches I recommend for a comprehensive psychological assessment for teenagers and young adults who have (or might have) autism. To help you use this approach, I am including some worksheets to help with keeping track of assessment information you collect with your clients. These are designed to keep all the information from an assessment together in one place so that you can have ready access to the information to help develop and revise your treatment plan as needed.

Previous Assessment Results

Use this worksheet to summarize the materials you obtained from previous assessments. You should try to gather all the previous assessment results here so that you can reference them in one place.

Client Name: _____

Assessment Instrument Name: _____

Type of Assessment Instrument: _____

Date of Assessment: _____ Age of Client: _____ Grade Level: _____

Summary of Results: _____

_____

_____

_____

_____

Assessment Instrument Name: _____

Type of Assessment Instrument: _____

Date of Assessment: _____ Age of Client: _____ Grade Level: _____

Summary of Results: _____

_____

_____

_____

_____

Assessment Instrument Name: _____

Type of Assessment Instrument: _____

Date of Assessment: _____ Age of Client: _____ Grade Level: _____

Summary of Results: _____

_____

_____

_____

Recent Assessment Results

Use this worksheet to summarize the results of assessment instruments you complete at the time you evaluate your client. Be sure to include the testing materials themselves in your clinical record.

Client Name: _____

Assessment Instrument Name: _____

Type of Assessment Instrument (circle one):

Autism Rating Scale   Parental Questionnaire   IQ Testing

Language Assessment   Adaptive Behavior Instrument

Executive Functioning Test

Other: _____

Summary of Results: _____

_____

_____

_____

Assessment Instrument Name: _____

Type of Assessment Instrument (circle one):

Autism Rating Scale   Parental Questionnaire   IQ Testing

Language Assessment   Adaptive Behavior Instrument

Executive Functioning Test

Other: _____

Summary of Results: _____

_____

_____

_____

Autism Questions

This is a sheet that includes all seven of the questions outlined earlier for an autism assessment. Write in your answers and the support you have for your answers in the space provided.

1. Is it autism?

_____

_____

_____

2. What is the individual's overall level of functioning (in terms of cognitive functioning, language ability and learning)?

_____

_____

_____

3. Are there additional diagnoses to consider?

_____

_____

_____

4. What behaviors and symptoms are most concerning the individual and/or family members?

_____

_____

_____

5. What are the most important targets for treatment?

_____

_____

_____

6. What community resources and recommendations are most important?

_____

_____

_____

7. What are the short-term and long-term prognoses?

_____

_____

_____

Clinical Summary

Use this worksheet to summarize your conclusions based on the assessment information you obtain. You would make these decisions based on assessment data you collect (both past and present), records reviews, clinical interviews, and other resources.

Notice that there is a section for Areas of Concern, both for clients and parents/guardians. One issue that will be addressed is the importance of considering what your teenage/young adult thinks they need help with. But also considering what the parent/guardian responsible for their care thinks needs addressed. You want to be sure to indicate that you are considering both perspectives when addressing treatment goals and interventions.

Client Name: _____

DOB: _____ Age: _____

Educational (grade level)/Employment Status: _____

_____

_____

Living Situation: _____

_____

_____

Diagnostic Impression: _____

_____

_____

If diagnosis is autism, discuss evidence of:

Social Difficulties: _____

_____

_____

Communication Difficulties: _____

_____

_____

Perseveration/Stereotyped Behaviors: _____

_____

_____

Symptoms of Other Diagnoses: _____

_____

_____

Intelligence Level (including IQ score, if applicable, and other evidence): _____
_____

Language/Communication Ability (include verbal/nonverbal and receptive/
expressive): _____

_____

_____

Strengths: _____

_____

_____

Weaknesses: _____

_____

_____

Main Areas of Concern (client): _____

_____

_____

Main Areas of Concern (parents/caregiver): _____

_____

_____

Prognosis: _____

_____

_____

Other Clinical Information to Consider: _____

_____

_____

chapter 3

Establishing Therapeutic Rapport

If you don't have a positive therapeutic rapport with a teenager or young adult in therapy, then that therapy is not going to be effective. Without positive rapport, there is no chance your client is going to listen to what you say. Without positive rapport, there is not a chance your client is going to put effort into any of your approaches. Heck, without positive therapeutic rapport, there is no chance your client is going to stay in therapy very long.

Teenagers and young adults with autism have the same need for developing therapeutic rapport as do any of your other clients. They also have the same ability to develop rapport. In fact, their ability to benefit from a positive therapeutic rapport, and benefit from therapy interventions, remains the same regardless of the severity of their autism symptoms (Puelo & Kendall, 2011).

I use a modified three-step process outlined by Bolton Oetzel and Scherer (2003) for developing therapeutic rapport. These are steps developed for establishing strong therapeutic rapport with teenagers and young adults in therapy. I modified them for use specifically for teenager and young adult clients with autism. The three steps are:

1. Presenting a positive and hopeful attitude
2. Emphasizing the adolescent's competence
3. Expressing confidence in the therapy process

Presenting a Positive and Hopeful Attitude

Before talking about this first step, it's important to understand the chief motivator for a teen or young adult. He (or she) wants independence. A teenager wants to be his own person. He wants to believe that he can be who wants to be. Up to this time, parents have been in charge of his life, and now he wants to start taking charge of his own life. No matter the diagnosis, level of functioning or intellectual ability, teenagers and young adults want their independence.

If a therapist or counselor is going to establish a positive working relationship with a teenager or young adult, they need to show they understand their desire for independence. The therapist needs to not only demonstrate this understanding but show that they are positive about it.

It is such a major part of what teenagers and young adults want that I truly believe there is no way they will respond positively to anyone who says they are "trying to help" if that person does not show they accept their independence. They need to be positive and show the teenager or young adult a hopeful attitude that gaining independence is a real possibility.

Now, this doesn't mean that you need to agree that the young person should have as much independence as he or she wants. And it does not mean that you need to work with him or her to start doing everything independently. You may very well disagree strongly with what the client thinks they should be able to do on his or her own. But disagreeing with the specifics of how much independence the client should have does not change the need for you to acknowledge, and show a positive and hopeful attitude about, that young person's need and desire to start becoming their own person.

I can say that every teenager and young adult with autism that I have worked with, from the lowest functioning to the most intellectually gifted individual, showed a strong desire to be independent. Each one had limitations, as we all do, and many had more limitations than the average person. But they all wanted their independence in whatever way they could get it. They all wanted to do the most they could on their own. Many times they were able to identify on their own how limited they were but still showed a desire to do things on their own to any degree possible.

Showing clear respect for a young person's need for independence and autonomy is essential for successful psychotherapy and counseling. One way of showing that respect is to start a discussion as early as possible about what the client is hoping to get from therapy. This means talking to the client alone and not just to the parents.

Depending on the client's level of functioning, this may be unexpected and even a little disturbing. She may be used to information and goals only coming from her parents. She may even prefer it be done that way. But treating the client in this way, as a person with individual opinions and goals, goes a long way towards showing a recognition of her desire for autonomy.

Parents often are the ones who bring teenage and young adult clients into therapy and counselors. They may be the ones who start off with identifying what the goals of therapy need to be.

Counselors and therapists working with young people often have to get this information from parents to know where sessions need to start. But getting information from just the parents is not going to establish rapport with the person with whom it is most important: the client. For this you need to get her view of the situation and her view of what needs to be addressed.

Following is an example of an introductory statement that can be helpful for working with a teenager or young adult with autism who is brought in by parents or caregivers:

> *Your parents told me what they are looking for here. And it all sounds very important. But I also wanted to hear from you what you hope to gain from our meeting. What do you think we need to work on? Where do you think you need to make changes?*

This part of the interview may have to be broken down into some more basic steps for clients who have intellectual disabilities. Here are some very basic interview questions that are helpful for those clients:

- Do you have friends?
- Are people nice to you?
- What things make you sad?
- What things make you angry?
- What things make you scared?
- Do you get in trouble sometimes at school?
- What were you doing when you got in trouble?
- Do you like talking to people?
- What causes problems when you talk to people?

Now, if you really want to make it clear that you are taking these types of things seriously, write them down. There is just something about writing down what someone says that shows you are taking them seriously. Teenagers and young adults particularly respond to this since they may be used to adults not listening so closely to what they say.

To help with this process, use the Goals Report by Client worksheet to guide you in what to ask and write down when asking about goals.

Goals Reported by Client

Fill out this worksheet as you talk with your clients. Use your client's words as much as possible.

Goal _____

_____

Behavioral Data Supporting Goal: _____

_____

_____

Is this similar to goal reported by parents/caregivers?   Yes   No   N/A

Goal _____

_____

_____

Behavioral Data Supporting Goal: _____

_____

_____

Is this similar to goal reported by parents/caregivers?   Yes   No   N/A

Goal _____

_____

Behavioral Data Supporting Goal: _____

_____

_____

Is this similar to goal reported by parents/caregivers?   Yes   No   N/A

Completing this worksheet with your teenage or young adult client shows that you are taking his views seriously. It takes the focus away from just doing what his parents, teachers or others say needs to be done and puts it on what he says needs to be done. This is the type of thing that really, really strengthens therapeutic rapport right out of the gate.

Emphasizing the Adolescent's Competence

Along with independence, adolescents and young adults want to feel positive about themselves. They want to believe they have the capability to take their lives in positive directions. Even if they recognize weaknesses, as well as strengths, they want to believe those weaknesses will not stand in the way of being the person they want to be. Severe intellectual limitations may interfere with what a person is able to do, but does not interfere with that person wanting to reach goals.

Having autism can be an obstacle to believing in yourself. Autism itself does not necessarily mean the person cannot reach goals. But hearing the word "autism" as it is used by many people can cause doubt. It is often used as a way of reflecting only limitations and inabilities. Being told you have autism can sound like the equivalent of being told you are incompetent.

Drummond (2013) summarized a good bit of research showing the importance of focusing on positive qualities of autism when working with adolescents with autism. Allowing the opportunity, from the beginning, for clients to talk about their strengths and their interpretations of what autism means to them shows that you are trying to recognize and acknowledge their competence. It shows them that you are trying to replace the negative ways they may have heard the word autism used throughout their lives.

In a detailed study of three high-functioning adults with autism, Hurlbutt and Chalmers (2002) found that these individuals were proud to have autism and did not want to see themselves as neurotypical. They wanted to be considered as experts in their own conditions and wanted to be consulted about what was addressed in their treatments. They also wanted to see themselves as unique. The authors suggested that addressing these topics at the very beginning of therapy is helpful for a positive therapeutic relationship.

Adolescents and young adults with autism tend to have a poor sense of identity compared to individuals without autism (Jackson, Skirrow & Hare,

2012). They want to see themselves in positive ways but are often held back by how others see them. They often lack a sense of who they are and a lack of understanding about what makes them distinct as an individual. When you ask about your client's understanding about autism, you open up the discussion about what is special about her. You set the stage to discuss how her differences may actually be areas of strength and competence.

For example, you can talk about how her differences related to social interactions are just that, differences. She may interact differently with other people, but that does not mean she is wrong. You can emphasize here that saying something is different does not necessarily mean right or wrong. This does not minimize problems but just underscores how it does not mean she is socially incompetent. Being different does not mean wrong or incompetent.

Helping teenagers and young adults develop a positive sense of what it means to have autism impacts whether they see their lives in positive or negative ways (Mogensen & Mason, 2015). Being a therapist who helps clients recognize the positive aspects of their lives, despite having a diagnosis that is often presented as negative, helps them develop a positive identity about themselves (Elfers, 2015). Embarking on this discussion right from the beginning of treatment sets the tone for your treatment and shows you acknowledge your clients' competencies in understanding themselves and what they want from their lives.

I realize that discussions on helping clients understand themselves may seem out of place if we are talking about clients with a lower level of functioning. But I would say it is lower-functioning clients who truly need to know someone appreciates their strengths and competencies.

No matter how impaired an individual might be, he still has hopes and goals. He wants someone to acknowledge the existence of the goals and abilities in order to reach (at least some of) them. It is the individual who is most looked on by others as not having abilities who is going to want even more for you to see abilities that are there.

Discussing areas of competence and strength right at the start also shows you recognize that your clients' views of themselves might be more positive than others' views. In a review of reports from 96 children with autism spectrum disorder, 211 controls and their parents, Egilson et al. (2017) found that teenagers with autism reported that they had better quality of life on four out of five dimensions than did their parents when rating them. These results highlight the importance of seeking the viewpoints of both clients and their parents, as your clients may be more willing and eager to see themselves in a positive light. This does not mean the parents do not care, but just may be less ready or able to see the strengths and competencies than the clients themselves.

Looking at areas of strengths and competencies also moves the discussion away from seeing your clients as having a disability. Being identified as only having a disability often leaves a person with autism feeling less human and feeling marginalized from the rest of society (Richards, 2016). Helping your clients move away from feeling this way about themselves can be helpful for establishing a positive therapeutic relationship right at the beginning of therapy or counseling.

Expressing Confidence in the Therapy Process

Making clear on the initial phone call that you are eager to help sets the stage for good rapport. Questions like "How can I help you?" or "What are you looking to change?" make it clear that you see the therapy and counseling process as geared towards making progress. You want everything you say to your client to have a sense of "I know that I can help you."

Providing a positive outlook that you can help your client with autism is important for establishing therapeutic rapport. This can be reflected with simple statements at the initial session like "I am going to help you with these problems" and "We are going to improve your social relationships."

Quality of life measures show that life satisfaction for adolescents with ASD is much lower than those without autism in the areas of friendships, leisure, and affective and sexual relationships (Cottenceau et al. 2012). If you present an attitude right from the start that therapy or counseling can help with these issues, then you are starting off at a very good place for helping establish rapport.

You want your statements during the initial session to reflect empathy ("I understand what you are saying"), support ("I recognize your strengths") and client-centeredness ("I want to focus on what you want in your life"). Showing evidence of empathy, support and understanding is important for getting effective therapy approaches off to a good start (Norfolk, Birdi & Walsh, 2007).

Clinicians who facilitate clients in talking about potential strengths and developing goals for treatment are taking a client-centered approach (Leach, 2005). This is the type of approach that can be most helpful for developing therapeutic rapport and leads to positive outcomes in daily functioning, increased client self-awareness of therapy goals and increased commitment to reaching those goals (Mulligan, White & Arthanat, 2014).

Setting Goals

As you obtain information from clients and, if necessary, parents/guardians, you then start translating it into treatment goals. You want to do that right from the beginning. You want to start as quickly as possible talking about goals so that you can share an attitude that therapy and counseling can make things happen.

Even if a client has been in therapy or counseling several times before, this does not mean that they found it helpful. Your client may have been through years of therapy or counseling but not really found anything he or she considered beneficial. Her parents may have noticed progress, but that does not mean she did. So, when you set goals with your client, do so from scratch without assuming that the goals set previously for treatment are going to be the ones she will want to have now.

The following worksheet is helpful for identifying specific ideas for goals to be set in therapy. This is set up as a therapeutic tool to help establish a positive working relationship at the very beginning of therapy. It makes very clear to the client that you want their input about goals and provides a guideline for setting those goals. Using this worksheet helps to address each issue that should be discussed when developing goals.

Client Goals

Use this worksheet to address each issue that should be discussed when developing goals with your clients.

Client Name: _____

Goal # _____

What behavior causes you the most problems? _____

_____

_____

When did this behavior last cause you a problem? _____

_____

_____

Can you give me an example of what happened when you had this problem?

_____

_____

_____

What would you like to be different? _____

_____

_____

How often do you think this type of behavior should be a problem for you?

_____

_____

_____

When completing this worksheet and discussing the first steps of therapy, you want to be conscious of the tone of voice you use. Your tone should show concern, support and consideration but not seem patronizing. This is particularly important for teenagers and young adults with autism seeking their own level of independence.

They may be used to others making decisions for them and may even have a level of resentment at the degree to which they know others need to make decisions for them. Your tone should reflect that you are looking to treat them as competent individuals as much as possible.

Using a supportive, respectful and serious tone when working with teenagers and young adults is particularly important for individuals who have more impairment. This could be in the case of social impairment or intellectual impairment. You need to provide clear and basic information, but also use a tone making it clear that you are not treating them as children. You should be sure to keep a respectful and adult tone even if you are being very basic in terms of what you are saying and how you are trying to explain things.

Continuing to keep this respectful tone will be important even if it is clear your client is not fully comprehending what you are saying. You may need to repeat things and repeat them in a way that is more basic and easily understood by the client.

If you need to, make it very clear that having to repeat what you say is not a problem. Continue to have the same respectful, serious and supportive tone you had prior to when you repeated what you were saying. Repeating material, even very basic material, should not change at all the level of respect and support that you have for the client and your tone of voice should reflect this continued respect and support.

Respecting Parents' Point of View

Finding the balance between respecting your client's views about what needs to be addressed in therapy and his or her guardian's views about what needs to be addressed is very important. It is often a good idea to explain to parents beforehand that you are going to talk to the client to get their opinion about what needs to be addressed. If the parent is the one who sets up the appointment, then you want to explain this over the phone.

During this phone call, discuss with the parent/guardian that you plan to talk with the client alone to get his opinion. Make clear that you will not necessarily take what their child says with 100% certainty regarding what needs to be addressed. Also, make clear you are trying to establish a positive therapeutic rapport by showing the client that you respect his point of view and want to know his point of view. Emphasize that you are not downplaying the parents' concerns, or the need to recognize their concerns, but are trying to get therapy off to a good start by making clear your respect for the teenager's or young adult's opinions.

Many individuals with autism have had parental involvement throughout their childhood and will still be facing similar difficulties to what they faced in childhood. Your client may not be ready to separate from parental involvement or may want more separation than her or his parents are willing to give.

Discussing with your client how much he or she wants to have the parents involved is one way of strengthening therapeutic rapport at the beginning of therapy or counseling (Reaven et al. 2012). You may not decide that having parents uninvolved, even if that is what he or she would prefer, is the most appropriate step to take. But just having the discussion can help get therapy or counseling started in a positive direction.

Perseveration & Therapeutic Rapport

It may be tempting to try and establish rapport with an individual with autism by connecting with their strong areas of interest. You may do well in terms of making a connection if you bring up topics of interest, but you may inadvertently cause more problems if you unwittingly feed into your client's perseverations.

Perseveration is a symptom that causes difficulties because the individual becomes very focused on the topic and has problems trying to focus on anything else. If you feed into this by helping to show a connection with their level of interest then you may be making the therapy problematic.

So, for example, if you have a client very focused on cars and you allowed her or him to talk about cars with no limits and no structure (e.g., he or she was just allowed to talk about cars for as long and as much as he or she wanted) then you would be doing nothing in session to help your client improve.

This would also be the case with a client who perseverated on a video game and you let them continue their intense focus with no limitations. It may be that your client would look happier with the therapy, and look happier with you, if you let him or her perseverate, but nothing would be accomplished. You would not really be improving therapeutic rapport, but would just be keeping your client from being challenged and getting upset.

But there are structured ways that you can use perseveration to help actually increase therapeutic rapport in therapy and counseling. Where this works best is when perseveration is used as a reinforcer for focusing on more therapeutic discussions. For example, if your client is told that she or he can discuss what they want after they have discussed a therapeutic topic for a set amount of time, then this can increase the likelihood he or she will participate in therapy.

Using perseveration as a reinforcer for participating in therapeutic discussions is supported in research. Baker et al. (1998) found that teenagers with autism showed motivation to engage more in discussing therapeutic topics if they were allowed to also address topics on which they perseverated. Perseveration was also used here as a reinforcer for more positive social behaviors.

Clients involved in this treatment showed increased interest in therapy sessions and happiness following the intervention. Vismar and Lyons (2007) also used perseverative behaviors as a reinforcer for getting youth involved in a behavioral training program. Charlop et al. (1990) found that using the perseverative behaviors as a reinforcer helped increase teenager and young adult participation in therapy sessions and did not increase the use of the perseverations later that day.

Let me tell my experience with a teenage client named April who had trouble staying in therapy. She would come into the session talking at length about her favorite book series. She would only want to talk about the books and would not put any effort into discussing the difficulties she had with schoolwork or getting along with her peers. Therapy sessions often seemed to be a waste of time because I could not get her to talk about any problems that had led to her coming into therapy in the first place.

Where I was able to get April to participate in the therapy sessions was when I stopped trying to get her to focus only on what we needed to discuss. When I gave the opportunity to talk about her book series for five minutes, provided she would then talk about what I wanted to talk about for five minutes, then I could get her to talk about the actual difficulties she was facing at home and at school.

Our agreement was a direct one where it was five minutes of her choosing what we talked about (usually her favorite book characters) and then five minutes of what I wanted to talk about (usually any difficulties her parents had reported that week). When we had this agreement in place I was able to spend at least half of each session on solid clinical work rather than spending the majority of each session telling April that she needed to focus on what we were supposed to be discussing during sessions.

Therapeutic Environment

When working with teenagers and young adults with autism you want a therapeutic environment that minimizes noises and distractions. Individuals with autism tend to do better in situations where they know what to expect and what is going to be addressed, so you will want to keep sessions consistent and structured.

You should also consider initially adding tasks that do not rely exclusively on talking. For example, providing an opportunity for your client to clarify what he is trying to say with drawings might be helpful. Art activities have been found to get adolescents with autism more engaged and conversational in therapy sessions than adolescents without autism (Martin, 2008).

You want the whole therapeutic environment that your teenage and young adult clients walk into to be one that is optimistic and supporting. Your client should recognize that she will be the focus in terms of identifying goals and direction but that parents or guardians may also play a supportive role, especially if that is what your client prefers.

Here the emphasis should be on the supportive role as you make clear that your client will take the lead as much as possible and appropriate. She will have the opportunity to express her goals and expectations as much as she wants but will also not be required to be in charge of the treatment any more than she feels comfortable. Taking these approaches increases your chances that the therapy or counseling will start off with a strong and effective therapeutic rapport.

chapter 4

Client-Centered Interventions

Last chapter I talked about developing positive therapeutic rapport and its importance for getting therapy off to a good start. In this chapter, I'm going to talk about keeping that rapport going and using it to create positive changes.

Maintaining positive rapport in counseling comes down to one word: trust. Your client needs to trust that the positive feelings you gave off at the beginning were not just a show. He or she needs to trust you are really, really trying to understand what she or he is going through. And your client needs to trust that you continue to believe that you can help.

Trust does not come easy for someone with autism. Autism leads to difficulties with social connections and those often result in negative responses. People leave when they get tired of trying to connect with a person with autism and get angry when his or her behaviors cause difficulties. Your client might connect with you at first, but will keep looking for proof that you are in this for the long haul. Making clear that you are not someone who bails on them when things get tough is key.

Recognizing, acknowledging and accepting doubts a client has about therapy is at the heart of the "client-centered" approach to therapy and counseling. You do not try to talk your client out of doubts but accept them as a way of showing support and positive regard. Then you continue to show that support and positive regard all the way throughout therapy. It is an approach that says "I know you have no reason to trust me or trust that I can help you. And I know it is my job to prove to you that I can help and that I do really care."

Basics of a Client-Centered Approach

In addition to developing trust, four other conditions are essential for client-centered therapy to create behavioral, emotional and personality changes. Carl Rogers, the founder of this approach, outlined these four conditions way back in 1957, but they remain as important today as they did then:

1. Two people (therapist and client) have to be in direct contact
2. Therapist has to have unconditional positive regard for the client
3. Therapist experiences empathic understanding of the client's experiences and seeks to communicate that understanding to the client
4. Communication of the empathic understanding and unconditional positive regard is done in an effective manner

Notice two terms are repeated in this list: empathic understanding and unconditional positive regard. Empathic means you work to understand the person's experiences and how that person sees the world. Positive regard means that you accept the person for who they are and recognize they have the ability to be the person they are meant to be.

Doing all this in an unconditional way (another term repeated in this list) means you maintain this approach regardless of what the client does or says in therapy sessions. You show that your understanding and your positive regard does not waver even when other people might have given up. Saying you are going to be someone who stays with your client to help them is essentially worthless. But when you show them that staying is what you are doing, you develop trust. And, when you have trust, positive regard and empathic understanding maintained unconditionally, then you have a chance for real therapeutic change.

Recognizing Strengths

Empathic understanding with someone who has autism means showing awareness that the very name autism carries negative meaning. It is a reflection of being different, and being different can be petrifying for a teenager or young adult. Taking a client-centered approach to autism emphasizes that different does not mean abnormal. Being different does not even mean being bad or negative. Different just means different, as in different abilities, different views and different strengths.

Teenagers and young adults with autism are often self-critical of their differences (Pfeiffer et al. 2013). They doubt that these differences relate to any type of strength or ability. As a result, they often have lower self-esteem than peers and a higher expectation that they will make major errors. They often see autism as just negative differences and problems and this contributes to a lot of negative self-image and self-doubt.

Identifying strengths for someone with autism is difficult but always essential for effective therapy and counseling. You can help by pointing out how some of the differences associated with autism can actually be sources of strength. For instance many individuals with autism have strong abilities to stay focused on tasks and continue that focus until they have tasks completed. Individuals with autism are also often not distracted by concerns about other people's opinions.

These are real strengths that are often not clear to people with autism or their families. Showing recognition and acceptance of these strengths, and sharing that recognition and acceptance during sessions, goes a long way towards showing unconditional positive regard.

I think of a story I read regarding a major financial advisor. He had a national reputation for making money for his clients when the housing bubble burst. Many people had investments in mortgages that ended up being nearly worthless, but this advisor had told his clients to stay away from those investments and to actually bet against them. His customers made money from those bets even while many other investors lost a great deal.

When I saw that advisor interviewed, he said that he had been diagnosed with autism. And then he went on to say that "I was not successful in spite of having autism. I was successful because I had autism." He went on to explain that, because he had autism, he was focused intensely on his tasks of finding ways to make money for his clients and to get as much useful information to his clients as possible so that they could make money.

He was not worried about making his clients happy, but was just focused on what he needed to do. So, when other advisors would say things that they thought would make their clients happy, he was focused only on giving them the facts, even if those facts made them upset. And so, his clients had more useful information to do what they needed to do for making a great deal of money while many other people were losing a great deal of money.

This is just one example of how some autism symptoms can actually be sources of strength and even sources of accomplishment.

Therapeutic Relationship

Many approaches to therapy and counseling with teenagers and young adults with autism focus on detailed and specific steps. And those can certainly be important, as we will see in later chapters of the book.

But there really is a weakness when these approaches emphasize the therapy steps and de-emphasize the need for a therapeutic relationship. Reading about these approaches in research journals or treatment manuals often suggests they can be effective anywhere and in any type of treatment environment. I don't agree with that and I don't think most therapists or counselors agree. There is a need for effective therapy steps but also a need for a deep, supportive and client-centered environment where those approaches are applied.

When taking this in-depth and client-centered approach to therapy with someone who has autism, there is a need to connect with that person as a full human being (Hobson, 2011).

You need to show that you have positive regard for your client as an individual, even if his or her behaviors and ways of looking at the world are different and sometimes challenging. Showing this throughout therapy helps to build the effective and positive relationship that is often missing from the paint-by-numbers approach emphasized in autism treatment manuals.

When addressing what is missing from those treatment manuals Christina Emmanuel (2015) put it well:

> *Reducing autism to behaviors fails to capture both what is essential about and what it is like to experience this condition.*

Here are specific suggestions for developing a deep, supportive and client-centered relationship for therapy and counseling with teenagers and young adults with autism:

- Be prepared to alter previously established processes and rules for therapeutic engagement (Koenig & Levine, 2011).
- Ask directed questions about clients' experiences, but allow them free reign to give their responses. Make clear that you are listening as they share their experiences.
- Emphasize that clients are free to, and encouraged to, talk about their experiences in ways that will not be judged or corrected. Show that the

sessions are focused around the client's subjective experiences and how they want to express those experiences (Tantam, 2000).

- Be directive with questions but nonjudgmental with responses.
- Show that you are listening actively to what your clients are saying.
- Listen and give feedback only when the opportunity presents itself to help the client understand how they are impacting their external world (Volmar, 2011).

In a client-centered counseling relationship, there is plenty of room for the client to describe what they are experiencing. Focus is on what the client has to say about themselves and not just what others have to say about them. There is plenty of room for the client to talk and not just for the therapist or counselor to talk.

Parental and familial input is respected, but not respected more than the client's input. Individual differences are accepted and treated as problems only if there is clear evidence they interfere with the client's functioning. There is a sense throughout everything the therapist or counselor says or does that there is no judgment and that the focus is helping the client be the best person he or she can be.

Teenagers and young adults with autism often experience a feeling of social deprivation that results in psychological stress similar to individuals who are actually socially deprived and isolated. They may have people in their lives who care very deeply about them and want to develop strong and positive relationships. But autism often leads these teenagers and young adults to feel isolated and to feel that others are not really trying to connect with them. They are not actually isolated or disconnected emotionally but they often feel as if they are.

Helping address these true feelings of isolation and emotional disconnect is why a strong therapeutic relationship is so important. Therapists and counselors need to combat these negative experiences of the world with in-depth and client-centered therapy and counseling goals. Some of the major goals for the in-depth and client-centered approaches outlined in this chapter include (Singletary, 2015):

- Providing an enriched environment where emotional support and social connections are emphasized
- Increasing opportunities for social and emotional connections
- Decreasing stress, anxiety and feelings of loneliness and isolation

At this point I want to make a brief mention of balancing structure and open-endedness when it comes to therapy and counseling sessions, because therapy and counseling sessions, especially those provided in a client-centered way, can veer off in one of two directions—and both of them have their problems. One direction is that it can all sound too planned, like the whole counseling and therapy process is all a series of very simplistic and well-defined steps that everyone has to follow. It can all start to look like what W. Silverman, back in the mid-1990s, called "paint-by-numbers psychotherapy".

But going off in an unstructured way isn't any more helpful. There is a whole lot that can be covered when you're working with someone with autism and having some specific plan for each session keeps them from becoming a mess. If you don't have some sort of structure each session can go off in a lot of different directions and nothing gets accomplished.

I recognize and appreciate full well that individuals with autism respond best to a good deal of structure. It is just that you do not want to emphasize structure at the expense of being able to help your clients really express who they are and what they are experiencing. And that makes a therapeutic relationship much, much weaker. Deciding how to work that balance is not an easy thing and requires a good deal of experience to figure out. If I am not sure if I am giving too many instructions during sessions, and not allowing the client room to talk, I will usually just ask (e.g., "I seem to be talking a lot here. Is there anything you want to bring up?").

Pre-Therapy for Lower-Functioning Clients

I realize that the client-centered approaches I outlined in this chapter require a good deal of verbal skills on the part of your client. But there is also a client-centered approach to therapy and counseling specifically designed for clients with much lower verbal skills.

Prouty (2001) developed this approach, called pre-therapy, as client-centered therapy used with low-functioning individuals, including individuals with autism. It provides structure that allows for the counselor to show understanding and empathy in nonverbal ways. It also involves a process that allows for development of an empathic environment in a way that does not depend exclusively on verbal language.

Pre-therapy involves steps where the counselor reflects back to the client some recognition of the client's reality. These steps are called reflections and Prouty lists four of them (as summarized in Carrick & McKenzie, 2011):

1. **Situation reflections:**
   - Therapist reflects some aspect of the immediate surrounding of both client and therapist. These would be aspects that the client may be conscious of and/or attentive to.
   - This does involve some very basic verbal behaviors.
   - These are verbal statements focused on reflecting the here and now.
   - These also reflect some reality that the counselor and client both share.
   - Examples include: "The sun is shining," "Somebody is speaking outside," "Your jacket is green," "It is very quiet."

2. **Body reflections:**
   - The therapist reflects the body posture or movements of the client. This could be either by bodily imitation, verbal reflection, or both.
   - Body reflections facilitate a more realistic body image.
   - Examples could include: "You are looking at the card board," "Your head is in your hands," "You get up, I get up" (while these things are actually occurring).
   - Other examples prompted by the therapist could include the therapist shaking his head and saying, "You shake your head" Or the therapist walking up and down the floor alongside the client and saying, "We walk up and down the floor."

3. **Face reflections:**
   - The therapist reflects what they see in the client's face, or the feelings they think they see expressed in how the client's face looks.
   - Face reflections address directly on mood and affect in the session.
   - This is a move towards expressing empathy by reflecting directly on something that is commonly addressed in a typical therapy session.
   - Utilizing this approach allows the therapy to reflect change in the client's feeling and address changes based on what is happening in the therapy session.

4. **Word-for-word reflections:**
   - Therapist reflects, word for word, on what the client has just said. For example, if the client says, "I need to get to school today," the therapist would repeat, "You need to get to school today." This

reflects to the client that the therapist recognizes the importance of what the client is saying. This can lead to the client expressing more about the importance of this issue.

- Here the focus is on what the clients says that seems to be the most important to the client.
- If the client is using words that do not make sense to the therapist, then the focus may have to be on words the therapist understands.

Brooks and Patterson (2011) showed the effectiveness of these types of reflections. This approach led to measurable increases in their clients' involvement in therapy sessions.

These reflections allowed for clients to improve how well they were able to express emotional pain and distress about unmet needs during therapy sessions. Field et al. (2001) also found earlier that individuals with autism showed increased social behaviors when contact reflections were used in therapy sessions. These studies reflect that the use of pre-therapy approaches help to create the supportive, client-centered environment that helps increase lower-functioning clients' involvement in therapy sessions.

Person-Centered Planning

One final topic I want to discuss here is called "person-centered planning." It is basically a means of incorporating client-centered approaches into team meetings about services. You could use this as a way of bringing about some meaningful change to those drab and lifeless meetings where major decisions are made about how best to help a teenager or young adult with autism.

In person-centered planning, the team focuses on trying to understand their client's vision of her or his future and what they would like to do with their life. Team members discuss services but it is always in the context of what goals their client has for his or her life.

This person-centered team meets to identify opportunities for their client (called the "focus person") to develop personal relationships, participate in their community, increase control over their own life, and develop the skills and abilities needed to achieve these goals.

Person-centered planning allows individuals with autism to participate more actively in their treatment planning than other types of team meetings (Hagner, Kurtz, May & Cloutier, 2014). There is much more of a focus on getting the client involved in the decision-making process. It is not a process of any one or group of individuals telling the client what they need, but it involves helping the client to communicate what he or she needs to make decisions and reach her or his goals.

As a counselor or therapist, you might be involved in person-centered planning for your clients. One way you can help your clients is to make sure the team is staying focused on what the client wants. Person-centered planning meetings can easily veer off into one or two members dominating the planning by saying specifically what they think the client needs.

Helping to keep this from happening, and helping to keep the team focused on what your client wants, is an important step you can take. You can also be the one to help the team best understand how to get your client involved as much as possible. Teenagers and young adults with autism often have difficulties speaking up in meetings, even ones that they know are being held for their benefit, and this may lead to others interpreting that they are not interested in being involved. Helping to make sure that all team members are using effective approaches for getting your client involved in the process is another way you can help with this planning.

chapter 5

Functional Analytic Psychotherapy Interventions

Therapeutic interventions for autism, as they are described in the scientific research literature, often seem empty to me. Oh, don't get me wrong, they address the various problems alright, and all the drab, empirical methods that are used to show that they work in the right way. You know, get 100 kids with social skills problems in a room and split them into groups of 50. Give one group a certain social skills training program and the other a different program and see which develops better skills.

These methods work, and the research results I just described support the approaches included in this book. But when I read about those interventions, sometimes there seems to be something missing. And it's not just the studies themselves that seem to be missing something. That sort of emptiness is also found in treatment manuals (which, I realize, applies to this book, since it can be considered one of those treatment manuals).

It took some time, but I was eventually able to put my finger on what was missing: there is no interpersonal aspect to them. There often seems to be a teacher-student aspect to the approaches rather than a therapist-client aspect. When the approaches are described, it often seems that the therapist is just talking to the client instead of working with the client.

Let's say you were teaching a teenager how to drive. You talk with them about driving, go over the specific steps and even use some visual aids to help them recognize what they need to do. You provide a set of instructions that they can go through each time they get in the car so they can be sure they are doing the right things.

All of those steps are important basic instructions for driving a car. Next you move to the part of the instructions in which the teenager gets into the car, and you show the teen all the parts and go through all the steps of getting ready to drive. You then start the car and continue going through the instructions. With the student behind the wheel, you continue to explain how to use the pedals, steer and so forth, saying, for example, "When you are in a car, you turn the wheel this direction to go one way and then that direction to go the other."

But you wouldn't stop there because there is something missing. What, you might ask? It is the part where you address what is happening in the moment. You are teaching someone to drive a car and they are driving a car while you are talking to them.

You wouldn't just say, "When you are in a car, you do this..." You would say "do this" while they are driving. Actually, what you probably do after a little bit of driving is say "That's what I mean" or "That's not quite right" after each major step. Your overall approach would not be to just provide general instruction, but to address the steps as they occur in real time. You would be addressing things the person does as they occur in the moment.

Now, I don't know about you, but the phrase "in the moment" is something I heard a lot in my initial therapy training. And I've continued to hear that phrase throughout the years at the many trainings and conferences I've attended. But for some reason, that phrase is not used when talking about therapy and counseling approaches for individuals with autism.

I don't know why that is the case, but there has been more of a focus on instructional approaches than on interpersonal approaches when it comes to autism interventions. One exception might be social skills groups, but even there the therapist/counselor is described more as a coach off to the sidelines rather than an actual participant in the game.

So, over the years I've looked for a therapeutic approach to autism that makes use of the therapeutic relationship itself as a tool for personal growth. In particular, I looked for an approach that made use, in the moment, of the difficulties that arose during the therapy sessions with my clients.

This therapeutic approach should be based on the fact that many problems with autism relate to interpersonal situations and that the therapy session itself is an interpersonal situation and so presents an opportunity for the individual to learn better ways of interacting.

I did find a number of references to this focus in the psychodynamic therapy (the modern term for "psychoanalysis") literature, and there are quite a lot of effective interventions in that literature. (Psychoanalysis fell out of favor with those working with clients with autism years ago because the early literature from 50–60 years ago erroneously blamed poor parenting as the cause of autism symptoms. That explanation was disproved after only a decade or so, and psychodynamic research since the 1970s clearly recognizes the neurodevelopmental causes of autism.)

The focus of modern psychodynamic research for autism is on the therapeutic relationship as a major factor in producing therapeutic change. Is it effective? Using case studies, the literature shows that psychodynamic techniques can be quite effective for helping teenagers and young adults. However, because the studies are case studies instead of large group studies, you will not typically run into them unless you are in an academic setting. This is because psychodynamic research articles are limited in scope, usually focusing on only one or two cases.

As a result, the findings are not considered applicable to the general population (and are not interesting). Whereas, positive findings from a well-designed, large study provide evidence that a therapeutic practice works in many or most cases, and so they get the publicity. Still, case studies are important because they can provide solid evidence for an intervention in a specific situation and provide the basis for larger studies.

In the end, psychodynamic research literature proved limited for my purposes of finding specific approaches to maximize the usefulness of therapy sessions. And that was because the articles usually made very little reference to what the therapist actually did.

The articles discussed meeting clients in the moment and recognizing the client for who they are and where they were at, but did not address specifically what the therapist was doing in sessions to make that happen. I was hoping for specific steps that therapists could take to accomplish some of the same things that were occurring in sessions these therapists and counselors described.

And I did find that in an approach called Functional Analytic Psychotherapy (FAP). It is considered a behavioral therapy approach, with its emphasis on behavior analysis, but is sometimes described as a fusion of behavior analysis and psychoanalysis. That description was what first caught my attention years ago.

Psychoanalysis and behavior analysis had always been presented to me as polar opposites of the therapy spectrum. Combining them would have been as if Sigmund Freud and B.F. Skinner were in a room together and came up with a therapy approach. I did not think that it could happen, but the FAP approach does accomplish it.

Functional Analytic Psychotherapy

FAP is based on the behavioral analytic approach to therapy and counseling (Kohlenberg & Tsai, 1994). FAP claims that people act the way they do because of contingencies of reinforcement that they experienced in past relationships. FAP says that psychotherapeutic change occurs when the therapist or counselor uses interventions and reinforcements to target more positive and effective behaviors.

Specifically, client improvement is brought about by the therapist or counselor noticing and responding effectively to client problems and improved behaviors as that occur during sessions. The client is taught about his behavior in the moment and then is able to take what they learned from the therapy session to use in their daily lives.

Although there had been a number of considerable research findings prior to the development of FAP that these principles can impact behaviors, before FAP, they had not been directly applied to the outpatient population (Tsai, Callaghan & Kohlenber, 2013).

There are five main rules to FAP. They are listed with explanations obtained from an article by Landes, Kanter, Weeks and Busch (2013):

1. **Watch for Clinically-Relevant Behaviors (CRB):** The core guideline for doing FAP is that a therapist should watch for clinically-relevant behavior (CRB). These are 1) in-session instances of the client's daily life problematic behavior (CRB1), and 2) improvements in behavior (CRB2).

   You are looking to immediately address any behaviors that are occurring in session that the client needs to change or that are examples of improved functioning. Many of the difficulties that clients encounter in outside relationships occur in session with their therapists, and many examples of behavioral progress occur in session as well.

2. **Therapy sessions should evoke CRBs:** While a therapy session involves

encouragement, trust, closeness and open expression of feelings, it does so in a time-limited setting where a fee is being charged and firm boundaries are set. This type of structure is likely to bring up clients' negative feelings and their difficulties with forming and maintaining interpersonal relationships. Therapists and counselors should watch for signs of these as the therapy process unfolds. These could either be problem behaviors that are the target of treatment (CRB1s) or positive behaviors that are evidence of progress (CRB2s). Therapists and counselors can evoke these behaviors with the typical interactions used during sessions or can try to more intentionally provoke these behaviors by focusing on the client's feelings and thoughts during specific moments during sessions.

3. **Reinforce CRB2s:** Whenever desired behaviors for handling social and/ or emotional difficulties are observed during the session, they should be reinforced. The method used to reinforce the behaviors should be based on what the therapist or counselor deems to be appropriate at the moment.

Typically, the reinforcement is given in the form of verbal praise. What is essential here is that it should be natural and not be set up as some sort of contrived plan on an artificial schedule.

4. **Observe the potentially reinforcing effects of therapist behavior in relation to client CRBs:** During the session, therapists should keep track of which reinforcers have the greatest impact (e.g., which situations lead to the greatest likelihood that positive behaviors will occur again). What you are looking to do here is find the most effective approaches during sessions for decreasing problem behaviors (CRB1s) and increasing more positive and effective behaviors (CRB2s).

5. **Give interpretations of variables that affect client behavior:** As you gain an understanding of the variables that impact your client's behaviors, you should pass along your discoveries to your client in a clear and direct manner. Keep in mind that the interpretation you give to the client does not provide any sort of additional benefit in and of itself. However, it *will* benefit a client if (and only if) they gain a clear understanding of what contributes to their behaviors and what sorts of situations they should watch for in the future.

FAP was developed as a way of applying behavioral analytic principles to the outpatient setting. It provides guidelines for therapists on how to notice behaviors, evoke behaviors, naturally reinforce effective client responses, and make important behavioral interpretations so that positive in-session changes can generalize to clients' daily lives.

The mechanism of clinical change in FAP—the essential ingredient to bring about client improvement—is that the therapist notice and respond effectively to client problems and improved behaviors as they occur during the session.

Use the worksheet CRB1 and CRB2 to keep track of CRB1s and CRB2s. Record specific information about CRB1s and CRB2s that come up during sessions. This is a worksheet that you would want to keep in a client's file, but keep it in a part of a file that you can get back to quickly—for easy reference. There is a place on this form for identifying the general reinforcers that are most effective for increasing positive behaviors. Use this section only for noting the very general types of reinforcers that seem to work. Most commonly these would include types of verbal praise when the client uses positive behaviors and when to specifically point out that the client is using effective behaviors. Be careful not to follow these reinforcers strictly, or to include too much detail about the reinforcers, because you want to make the reinforcers you use during sessions naturally occurring whenever possible.

You can have a plan for the type of reinforcement likely to be effective but you really want to let the specific statements that you make be ones that seem appropriate in the moment. These are the types of natural reinforcers that are most likely to increase the chances that positive behaviors will occur more often in the future.

Following are two case examples of using FAP approaches in therapy with a teenager and a young adult with autism:

Case Study
CRB1 vs. CRB2

Ellen is a high school senior who was diagnosed with autism when she was in elementary school. One of the difficulties that led her into therapy as a high school student was that she felt socially alienated. She talked about not having any friends and about having difficulties getting along with peers. She specifically came into therapy stating that she wanted to make progress with social skills. She identified poor social skills as an issue causing her considerable amounts of emotional distress.

When she met with the therapist, it was clear that Ellen was having difficulty with maintaining eye contact, perseverating and not showing any clear interest in what the other person was saying.

During the second session, the therapist pointed out to her when these three specific behaviors occur. This involved the therapist pointing out to Ellen when she would listen to the therapist talk but look up in the air or down at the ground. Her therapist also pointed out when Ellen would start talking about subjects that were not directly related to what was being discussed during the session and noted when Ellen did not look like she was interested in what the therapist was saying. This would particularly involve Ellen giving no response to what the therapist said or not leaning forward to reflect interest in what the therapist was saying.

Each of these behaviors were pointed out as CRB1s and the therapist noted to Ellen each time they occurred. Pointing these behaviors out was followed by the therapist suggesting specific behaviors that Ellen could use as a way of decreasing the frequency of these CRB1s.

These more positive behaviors were identified as CRB2s and they were brought up as suggestions by Ellen's therapist and then were reinforced with positive verbal statements when they occurred during sessions. These CRB2s included Ellen maintaining eye contact while the therapist was talking to her, responding in a way that was relevant to things that the therapist talked about (rather than subjects Ellen wanted to talk about) and leaning forward and making verbalizations like uh-huh as a way of reflecting interest in what the person was saying.

As these behaviors were addressed, the frequency of these CRB2s increased to a noticeable degree by the fourth session. Following the fourth session Ellen was given the homework assignment to use these more positive social behaviors when she interacted with other people outside of session and report on their effectiveness during the next session.

Example

CRB1 and CRB2 Example

CRB1 (Target Behavior): Looking away when person is talking

CRB2 (Positive Replacement Behavior): Maintaining eye contact while person is speaking

Effective Reinforcer (be specific): Pointing out when CRB2 occurs and reminding her that this is the positive behavior discussed earlier

Case Study

CRB2 and Anger

Larry was a young adult who worked at a local grocery store. He had been diagnosed with autism spectrum disorder when he was in middle school and had been in a vocational training program through the autistic support department at his high school.

Larry had come into therapy because he was getting into fights and loud arguments with his coworkers when they did not do things specifically the ways that he thought they should do them. Larry's response to these problem situations involved raising his voice and repeating his demands about what he thought needed to be done. These were the behaviors that were identified as CRB1s during the second session.

During the third session, Larry told his therapist about an incident in which a coworker told Larry something that Larry disagreed with. The therapist stated that he could see the other person's point of view. When this happened, Larry started to raise his voice and stated twice how he could not accept that the therapist agreed with this other person. Before Larry started yelling, the therapist pointed out specifically to Larry that he was raising his voice and that he was talking repetitively about not liking what the therapist said.

Larry stopped and said that he did not notice that he was doing this. He acknowledged that what the therapist did made him angry, but he had not noticed that he was starting to raise his voice and repetitively talk about what he was upset about. Larry's therapist worked with Larry on a specific sentence that Larry could state when he disagreed with what the therapist said. Specifically, Larry was asked to say "I am really angry about what you said there because I do not agree with it."

Larry continued to raise his voice and talk repetitively about situations that bothered him over the next several sessions and this was pointed out to Larry. He was encouraged each time to make statements about how he felt without raising his voice. By the eighth session the therapist had reinforced this CRB2 four times as Larry was expressing his anger about things that were discussed during session. He had been taught to use this behavior when facing difficulties at work, but following the eighth session he was assigned to keep track of specific situations in a notebook where he used the CRB2 verbal behavior as a way of dealing with anger.

He was able to report at the next session at least eight different situations where he was able to keep himself from yelling and talking repetitively about something someone had done by relying on verbal statements made directly to the person about being angry at what they said. It would not be accurate to say that in each of those situations the other person responded positively, but at least it kept each of the situations from becoming situations where Larry would get into trouble.

CRB1 and CRB2 Example

CRB1 (Target Behavior): Raising voice (starting to yell)

Additional CRB1: Repetitive statements about what another person did (Note: This additional CRB1 is handwritten in this section since both relate to the same CRB2.)

CRB2 (Positive Replacement Behavior): Verbal statement about feeling angry about what another person did

Effective Reinforcer (be specific): Verbal praise

Self-Monitoring

FAP relies on behavioral analytic principles to support its therapeutic approach. It also relies considerably on the behavioral therapy intervention of self-monitoring. Using CRB1s and CRB2s in session is done as a way of increasing the individual's self-monitoring of behaviors in interpersonal situations. Given the importance that self-monitoring plays in FAP, I thought it would be useful to take a look at the research on the effectiveness of this intervention for individuals with autism.

Epstein, Siegel and Silbermen (2008) reviewed what cognitive neuroscience has found regarding self-monitoring. They defined self-monitoring as the ability to attend, moment by moment, to one's action. Self-monitoring requires motivation and attentiveness. They note that there are three types of attention involved with self-monitoring:

1. Alertness—readiness to respond to anticipated stimuli
2. Orienting—selecting information that is relevant in a situation and ignoring other information
3. Executive abilities—management of unanticipated stimuli (conflicts, errors, decisions) that reach the person's awareness; this requires overcoming habitual action

Hume, Loftin and Lance (2009) identified self-monitoring as a psychological intervention that can help increase independence among individuals with autism. They identified self-monitoring as the process by which the individual is taught to discriminate and make a record of the occurrence of a target behavior. They also identified self-monitoring as an element of self-management, which they defined as the person monitoring their behaviors and using specific approaches to help change their target behaviors.

Their research reviewed several studies where self-monitoring was used successfully to address behavior problems in individuals with autism. Many of these studies involved children, but there were some that involved adolescents.

Tiger et al. (2009) outlined steps of self-monitoring that came down to two very general steps:

- Teach the client to observe and detect instances of target behaviors.
- Teach the client to deliver reinforcement according to arranged contingencies.

They discussed these steps in a research article where they taught a 19-year-old man with Asperger's disorder to self-monitor during a behavior therapy procedure. Specifically, he was taught to set a timer, reset the timer following instances of skin picking, and place a ticket into an envelope when the timer sounded if no instances of skin picking had occurred. This study showed that self-monitoring within behavior therapy could be effectively implemented and decreased the necessity of having practitioners involved in the behavioral procedure.

Grynzpan et al. (2012) studied whether self-monitoring approaches could be used to increase the effective use of appropriate eye contact by adolescents with autistic disorders in social situations. They studied these factors following their conclusion that atypical visual behaviors account for much of the social misunderstanding in autism. They studied 14 adolescents and young adults with autistic disorder and 14 typically-developed teenagers and young adults. These authors found that self-monitoring approaches could be used to increase visual gaze and that the approach also increased scores on a measure of social understanding.

Each of these scholarly articles addresses the basic aspects of self-monitoring and shows the potential benefit that self-monitoring presents for individuals with autism. Behavioral therapy often relies on self-monitoring for helping clients make behavioral changes. Even individuals with autism and intellectual disability have shown in research studies, like those reviewed here, that they can use self-monitoring to make behavioral improvements.

FAP offers a therapeutic approach where self-monitoring is stressed in the session and offers a way to then transition the use of self-monitoring for addressing behaviors outside of session. This will be important for implementing the specific behavioral approaches for social skills, emotion regulation and perseveration that I will address in the next several chapters.

CRB1 and CRB2

Client Name: _____

CRB1 (Target Behavior): _____

_____

CRB2 (Positive Replacement Behavior): _____

_____

Effective Reinforcer (be specific): _____

_____

CRB1 (Target Behavior): _____

_____

CRB2 (Positive Replacement Behavior): _____

_____

Effective Reinforcer (be specific): _____

_____

CRB1 (Target Behavior): _____

_____

CRB2 (Positive Replacement Behavior): _____

_____

Effective Reinforcer (be specific): _____

_____

chapter 6

Social Skills Training

One of the reasons I wrote this book is that there isn't a book that has all these interventions in just one place. There's a bunch of books for kids, but none for teenagers and young adults (that's also the case with research—lots on kids, not so much for older individuals). I'll start here with the interventions researched the most: social skills training.

Social skills problems are the most common reasons that teenagers and young adults with autism (or their families) seek out psychological services. Your potential clients may not be the ones who are seeing problems but they may have been told to seek out counseling by family members, teachers or even bosses. And if these people are telling them to get help, you might see quite a bit of anxiety, depression, anger—or all three.

Providing social skills training for teenagers and young adults is much more difficult than for children. That's because social situations become more complex and multifaceted as people get older. Teenagers and young adults respond to their peers in so many different ways that it can be difficult to predict which types of social interactions your client will run into.

Childhood social interactions tend to follow a scripted set of directions. With children, you pretty much use the same set of social steps regardless of who they're interacting with. What they say to one kid is pretty much the same as what they're going to say to another kid. That's why there's a whole bunch of short social stories children's books with nice pictures that show specifically what to do when they meet another child.

However, teenage and young adult social interactions follow a set of if-then statements. Teenagers in particular are unpredictable and there can be a lot of different rules for different situations that can change based on who they are trying to interact with.

Now, this doesn't mean that you give up on trying to help your teenage and young adult clients establish some rules for social interactions. In fact, establishing social scripts, where specific rules are set for social interactions, is one of the main interventions I talk about here. It is just that you want to gear your interventions to helping clients to recognize and navigate the complexities they'll face when interacting with other people.

Providing focused interventions that are combined with flexibility and emotional support is really, really important for helping teenagers and young adults benefit from socials skills interventions.

Session Structure

Below is a structure for a client session that has enough flexibility to provide social skills interventions, and that can be adapted to address other problems.

Here is a general outline for each counseling or therapy session:

- Review any specific problems or changes that have occurred since the last session (this is the part where family or friends will participate).
- Decide which issues should be discussed during the session (depending on the situation, this will be before or after family or friends leave).
- Once an agreement has been reached about what is to be discussed, discuss a specific example of when the client had the problem being addressed (most often this will involve an incident that occurred since the last session, but it could be one brought up during earlier sessions).
- If the discussion is carried over from the previous session, briefly review what was covered during the last session and where the discussion left off.
- If there was a homework assignment from the previous week, this would be a good time to review it.
- Use client-centered approaches throughout the session (including pre-therapy approaches for less verbal clients) to strengthen therapeutic rapport.
- While reviewing past incidents and deciding on the topics to address this session, look for opportunities to address the client's behaviors in the session. For example, if the client is using poor social skills while talking, point this out and prompt them to change behaviors based on what had been discussed in previous sessions.
- Introduce the skills training you will use in this session to address the specific issues that were agreed upon.
- Practice the use of these skills. With social skills this will involve

practicing social scripts. (Most likely your client will have had this sort of training as a child and will be familiar with the format.) Go through role-playing exercises discussing how the skills can be implemented. Model the use of skills that might cause your client difficulties.

- Discuss real-world scenarios where your client could use these skills. Identify possible difficulties that could arise and suggest plans that your client can use for overcoming these difficulties. This is where the discussion of if-then approaches might come in (e.g., "IF the other person acts this way THEN take these steps; IF the person acts a different way THEN take these steps").

- Create an assignment that lets your client practice skills before the next session. If appropriate, review assignments with family members or friends who will help the client with practicing skills.

Notice how this approach combines different elements that I discussed in previous chapters. It allows for you to establish the client-centered approach that I emphasized, but also allows for the structure that works well with individuals who have autism. There also is room for changing course if your client brings up something new or is showing unexpected challenges.

Social Skills Introduction

When you move into introducing social skills training for therapy and counseling sessions, your clients or their parents may ask why social skills are a problem in the first place. You are going to want to have some sort of explanation ready.

Social skills are a problem for individuals with autism because they do not process social interactions the same as everyone else. Connecting with people and responding to people do not come as naturally for someone with autism as they do for someone without it. This often causes individuals with autism to look strange or to look rude. They may look as if they do not care about other people or are not particularly interested in other people. None of the above impressions are true.

Individuals with autism are different, as opposed to strange, with respect to how they relate to other people and in the ways they express themselves in social situations. People with autism do care about other people and are interested in other people. This is why they experience loneliness and embarrassment. If teenagers and young adults truly did not care about other people, then they would not care enough to feel lonely or be embarrassed at how they are coming across.

There are several different theories about why people with autism come off as socially disconnected and socially awkward. One of the most common theories relates to what is called Theory of Mind. This theory essentially states that what is lacking in autism is the ability to put oneself into someone else's shoes. People with autism, the theory goes, do not connect socially the same as other people because they are unable to consider what the other person might be thinking or feeling.

As a concept, Theory of Mind is best explained by what is called the Blue Bunny Story. This exercise is particularly relevant for explaining autism to parents of children, but it is such a clear explanation of Theory of Mind that I use it for teenagers, young adults and their parents as well. There are many variations of this story, but it essentially lays out the social difference between individuals with autism and those without it. I turn the story into an exercise. First I tell the Blue Bunny Story and then I ask my client a question. Here's the story:

Blue Bunny Story

Fred is being given a test. He is shown a blue stuffed bunny in a room where there are two hats on a table. One hat is red and the other is green. The man giving Fred the test takes the bunny and puts it under the red hat. Fred is then asked to leave the room. After he leaves the room, the man takes the blue stuffed bunny from the red hat and moves it to under the green hat. Fred is then asked to come back into the room. He is then asked where he thinks the bunny is.

Following the story, I ask my client, "What hat does Fred pick?" Typically, individuals with autism will pick the green hat while those without autism will pick the red hat. Why is this? The individuals with autism will not see that Fred couldn't have known that the bunny was moved because he wasn't in the room. They cannot put themselves in Fred's shoes in terms of recognizing what Fred would see. Since they know the bunny was under the green hat they expect that Fred should know it as well. They are seen as lacking the Theory of Mind that allows them to recognize Fred's perspective.

Theory of Mind is probably the most well-known of several theories of social difficulties in autism. What is common among all of these theories is that people with autism lack the very basic skills that are used to positively interact with people and that lead to social connections. A person with autism may be interested in social connectedness, but the skills to successfully engage in it are lacking. Learning these skills is the focus of many types of autism treatment.

Now, you could very easily argue that what causes difficulties for someone with autism is not that the individual wants social relationships but, rather, that the individual is *expected* to want social relationships. It may very well be that teenagers and young adults with autism would be just fine if people would stop demanding that they have a lot of social relationships. Because really, people who have lots of social relationships are often still miserable. And this is a valid point of view.

In fact, as we will discuss in the next chapter, putting an emphasis on having friends can be problematic for autism treatment, and in many cases, it can be damaging. I have seen many cases where a teenager or young adult with autism is very depressed or anxious NOT because they do not have friends, but because they have been told so often that they HAVE to have friends.

They were comfortable with how many people they did, or did not, interact with. But they were distressed by how often they were told things like "You don't have enough friends" or "You don't get around other people enough" by people who really mattered to them.

When it comes to addressing social skills with someone who has autism, you really want to make sure you are taking a balanced approach. Social skills interventions should focus on learning effective skills for interacting with people that your clients can make use of when needed. Once your clients have learned important social skills, and can use them comfortably, the "when and how" they choose to use the skills should be up to them.

You want to use these new skills to try and make some new friends? Fine. You want to use these skills just to be more comfortable talking to a few people at work? Fine. You want to use these new skills so you can feel more comfortable asking for help at the grocery store? Fine.

Your message to the client should be: "I'll help you learn the skills and then we'll decide what is best for you about when you use them."

Social Skills Scripts

One of the most common approaches in social skills training is the use of "scripts." These scripts are sets of steps that the individual can use when faced with certain situations. Scripts follow the rules of engagement for handling social interactions and spell out the specific behaviors needed at each stage in the social interaction. When individuals with autism are comfortable with these scripts, they can approach social situations effectively and may not even look different from someone who approaches social situations more naturally.

Social skills scripts are often described as being beneficial only for individuals who are higher functioning and can follow the detailed rules associated with social interactions. But there are a number of behavioral studies showing effective use of social skills scripts for teenagers and adults who are much less verbal than the average person with autism. The studies suggest modifying the details that are provided for each script step and the manner in which each step is explained.

Typically, lower-functioning individuals will need steps that are more basic (usually just one very specific step at a time) and that are described in ways that are more direct and easier to follow.

Below is a modified version of the social skills used in the Gaylord study. It was used to help improve the social skills of a 17-year-old high school student diagnosed with autism and intellectual disability (called "mental retardation" at the time) and for a 20-year-old adult who also attended the same high school and was diagnosed with both autism and severe intellectual disability. They were both involved in a study where a version of this script was found to help improve their peer interaction skills.

Social Skills Training Script

Step 1:   Say, "Hi."
Step 2:   Ask "How are you?" and wait for other person's response (usually they will say "fine" or something similar).
Step 3:   Ask, "Want to play my computer game?" (Note: In the original study, it was a handheld version of Pac Man.)
Step 4:   Turn on game.
Step 5:   Hand game to other person.
Step 6:   Watch while other person plays and offer encouragement.

Step 7:   Other person plays game until it is over.

Step 8:   Other person hands game back.

Step 9:   Read other person's score.

Step 10:   Play your turn on the game.

Step 11:   Read your own score at the end of the game.

Step 12:   Offer to play another game.

Step 13:   Play game or other person says, "No thanks."

Step 14:   Say, "Good game."

Step 15:   Say, "Bye."

You can see here how social skills scripts work. Each step of the social interaction is spelled out for the person to follow. In this case, each step was very basic and direct as a way of making it usable for two individuals with both autism and intellectual disabilities. This script was set up in a way that a teenager or adult with autism could follow each step.

To come up with the previous script, the researchers involved in the study combined their observations of students at the local school with what they knew about how individuals interact with each other. And that is how you can approach social skills scripts in your own clinical work.

Social scripts work for clients of all abilities. Developing them can take some time and usually is an individual process. I provided the prior example above just to show what a social script typically looks like. But I really do not recommend using a premade script. In my opinion, scripts that are too much of the one size fits all variety are of limited use when trying to help a teenager or young adult with the unique situations that are causing him or her difficulties.

What I prefer is using a structured process where you work with your client on developing scripts that address the specific types of situations causing her or him problems. Here's the process I recommend. With your client's help, identify the types of situations that are causing them difficulties.

Next, select from those three situations where your client is having difficulties. For each of these, identify where they had the problems. Review these situations and come up with specific steps your client could have used to handle the situations more effectively. List these as a series of steps that your client can use to handle similar situations effectively in the future. You can outline the steps similar to the way that the steps were outlined in the previous sample.

The Problematic Social Situations worksheet (page 79) can be used to obtain information about the problematic social situations that you can use for developing social skills scripts.

Problematic Social Situations

Talk with your client about three social situations that caused them problems within the past two weeks. Write there responses on this worksheet.

Client Name: _____

1st Situation

Who was involved?

_____

_____

What was the situation?

_____

_____

What did you say or do?

_____

_____

What did the other person say or do?

_____

_____

What were the worst parts of the situation?

_____

_____

2nd Situation

Who was involved?

_____

_____

What was the situation?

_____

_____

What did you say or do?

_____

_____

What did the other person say or do?

_____

_____

What were the worst parts of the situation?

_____

_____

3rd Situation

Who was involved?

_____

_____

What was the situation?

_____

_____

What did you say or do?

_____

_____

What did the other person say or do?

_____

_____

What were the worst parts of the situation?

_____

_____

Social skills scripts for teenagers and young adults need to contain room for different alternatives. That is simply the only way to address the variety of responses that your clients may get from different individuals. One of the reasons that it is useful to develop scripts based on your clients' personal experiences, as opposed to pre-written scripts, is that it allows you to address the situations and alternatives that are most likely to impact your clients.

You can use the situations your client gives to you so as to start developing scripts based on what your client is likely to face out in the real world. You are taking their individual experiences and not expecting they are going to be facing the same situations as everyone else (including everyone else with autism).

Visually, what this will look like is that each step in the script you create for social situations will have a large space (five or six blank lines) underneath it. It is in those spaces that you will write the different alternatives that might occur at that step.

Take, for example, Steps #1 and Steps #2. That is OK. But it assumes the other person responds in an appropriate way. What if they don't? What if their response is "Get away from me!"? It is not nice to think about, but it is a very real possibility. Or what if the person does not just respond "Fine," but asks a question back ("Fine. How are you")? Or what if the other person does not recognize your client and asks who they are? These are just some examples of the different types of responses that a teenager or young adult might face in different situations.

Filling in the blanks with alternative responses is done in a number of ways. Ideally, you would come up with the different possibilities and responses by brainstorming with your client.

You would role-play different responses from the other person and then role-play how your client might respond. This would allow for discussions about social situations your client faces and would help them connect even more to the different steps on the script. But there may be too many alternative responses to be discussed in one session and you simply might not have enough time.

So, providing your own insights about what the alternative responses might be is acceptable as long as you review the steps with your client. You can say, "Here is one possibility that I know could occur." When you provide your suggested response, you can ask, "What do you think of that response?" as a way to get your client's input.

Not all social interactions work out well, and so it can be useful to help clients determine when it is time to stop pursuing a conversation and walk away. As an example, I developed a series of steps called "Deciding When to Bolt" that I use to outline the thinking process the individual takes when it is time to give up (or "bolt") on an attempted social interaction:

- Say, "Hi, what is your name?"
- If the person does not answer, attempt the question again.
  - o If the person still does not answer, say, "Well, it was nice to meet you," and walk away.
  - o If the person responds with an angry statement or insult, say, "Wow, that was really not nice. I don't want to talk with you anymore," and walk away.

Once you have developed a set of social skills scripts, some ways to strengthen your client's ability to use them include (Gresham, Sugai & Horner, 2001):

- Role-playing exercises (to address gaining skills in specific problem situations)
- Modeling (therapist exhibiting how approaches are to be used)
- Behavioral rehearsals (using skills in session when interacting with therapist)
- Performance feedback (specific comments from therapist about social skills effectiveness)
- Weekly socialization assignments

Social Behaviors

Determining what specific social behaviors need to be addressed for an individual client can be a daunting task. Social skills training can address a large number of difficulties, but not all of your clients will have the same types of problems.

On the following page is a list that can be used to identify which types of behaviors to work on in social skills training. Use the list, along with material you have from you client's self-reports, your observations of the client's behaviors and your review of any records you have about your client's behaviors, to identify, and then prioritize, areas to work on.

Problem Areas for Social Skills

Circle specific items related to each category that the client shows during session or reflected in self-reports of problematic social situations.

Client Name: _____

Conversational skills

• Talks too softly

• Talks too quickly

• Looks down when talking

• Looks away when talking

• Has poor eye contact when other person talking

• Other: _____

_____

Trading information

• Focuses only on one topic

• Shows no evidence of being interested in what other person is saying

• Does not verbally respond when other person says something

• Responds with an irreverent (off-topic) remark

• Gives no relevant response to questions

• Other: _____

_____

Choosing appropriate friends

• Calls peers "friends" who are clearly mean or bullies

• Calls peers "friends" despite having little interaction with them

• Identifies individuals as "friends" who are much too young or too old for them

• Chooses "friends" who are bad influences

• Other: _____

_____

Appropriate use of humor

- Tells "jokes" that no one would think are funny

- Says something is a "joke" when others would clearly take it seriously

- Laughs at situations that are clearly serious

- Laughs when someone gets hurt

- Says "it's only a joke" in situations where others would clearly be hurt

- Uses crude humor in inappropriate situations

- Other: _____

_____

Entering a conversation

- Interrupts others without waiting for appropriate pauses

- Talks about subjects not relevant to what others are saying

- Starts into a conversation with no indication of being invited

- Yells as a comment to what someone else says in conversation

- Other: _____

_____

Exiting a conversation

- Walks away from conversation without an appropriate exiting statement

- Makes comment about being "bored" or "just not wanting to talk anymore"

- Yells or screams and walks away

- Continues talking even if it is clear that other people are not interested

- Talks abruptly about a topic different from what others are discussing

- Other: _____

_____

Good sportsmanship

• Has problems taking turns

• Shows difficulties following rules

• Shows difficulties accepting rules of games

• Gets angry and yells when losing

• Ends game angrily if losing

• Makes negative statement to opponent about winning or losing

• Walks away if the game is not going in a way they want

• Other: _____

_____

Handling teasing and bullying

• Cries loudly and continuously if bullied

• Stays in situations when clearly bullied

• Shows no recognition of being teased or bullied

• Does not report bullying to parents or teachers

• Other: _____

_____

Handling disagreements

• Yells and screams whenever others express disagreement

• Expresses disagreement and walks away

• Calls person names when expressing disagreement

• Yells about situations not being "fair" when expressing disagreement

• Other: _____

_____

Next is a list of specific positive social skills that can be used to improve problem areas. Notice the headings in this list are the same as the problem behaviors list. Using these two lists together, you can first identify specific problem behaviors to address and then select positive social skills to replace those problem behaviors.

Positive Social Skills

Listed below are some positive social skills that may need to be address during session. Consider when these are specific areas that need to be addressed with your client.

Client Name: _____

Conversational skills

- Talk in a clear voice
- Use appropriate volume when talking
- Speak to others in appropriate rate of speech
- Maintain eye contact when talking with other person
- Use clear annunciation when talking

Trading information

- Keep on topic
- Do not stay on one topic (unless others are doing the same)
- Change topics if others change topics
- Make verbal statements showing interest
- Say something if other person says something
- Make relevant statements to what others say

Choosing appropriate friends

- A friend is not someone who bullies you
- Friends are people you have more than periodic contact with
- People who interact with you because of their jobs may be nice but are not necessarily friends
- Friends are usually people close to your own age

Appropriate use of humor

- Recognize that jokes should not hurt people

- Jokes should be funny (learn better jokes)

- If people take what you say seriously, it is not a joke

- Just calling something a "joke" does not make it a joke

- Crude humor is only appropriate in certain situations

Entering a conversation

- Wait for appropriate pauses before starting to talk during a conversation

- Identify topics others are talking about before joining a conversation

- Stay on-topic when joining a conversation

- Do not yell or become disruptive to join in a conversation

Exiting a conversation

- Make statements like "I have to go now" or "Have a good day" when exiting a conversation

- Do not comment that you are "bored" or "just do not want to talk anymore" when exiting

- Do not yell or scream when exiting because of disagreement

- Recognize if you try talking to someone and they do not respond or show interest you should walk away

Good sportsmanship

- Make sure someone takes a turn after you do

- Follow the rules set for the game

- If you are agreeing to play a game, you need to follow rules

- If you do not understand the rules of the game, ask

- Do not yell or scream if you are losing

- Losing is not a terrible thing as long as you tried your best

- Do not brag when winning

- Do not call the other person names when losing

- Do not yell or cry when losing

- Stay with the game until it is over even if you are losing

Handling teasing and bullying

- Do not just stand around and cry if you are being bullied

- Tell a teacher or parent if you are being bullied

- Leave the situation if you are being bullied

- Learn what being "bullied" means and how to recognize it

Handling disagreements

- You do not need to yell and scream if you disagree with someone

- Stay and express disagreement with someone rather than walking away

- You can walk away if the other person starts being mean or starts yelling

- Do not call other people names during disagreements

- Just because you disagree with someone does not mean they are being unfair

Here's a summary of the process:

1. Identify the specific problem areas that need to be addressed on the list of problem behaviors.

2. Select positive social skills from the second list to counter the problem areas.

3. Create one or more scripts that incorporate the positive social skills so that your client gets practice using them, and learns to resolve their problems.

4. Use the scripts within the session. You can incorporate role-playing, modeling and behavioral rehearsal exercises for emphasizing the use of positive social behaviors with feedback provided during sessions to help your clients see how effective they are being with using positive social behaviors.

5. Give your client assignments to ensure they are using the social behaviors outside of sessions.

Social Skills Groups

Up until now, we have focused the discussion of social skills training in individual therapy and counseling. But social skills groups are also a useful treatment modality. There is actually quite a bit of research supporting the effectiveness of this approach for helping teenagers and adolescents with autism. And social skills groups also offer the opportunity for real-world applications of positive social skills.

Putting together a social skills group can be somewhat challenging but no more than is the case with other group therapy programs. One difficulty that may be present with an autism group, compared to groups to address other conditions, is that you may get more variability in terms of communication skills and intellectual ability.

There may be some individuals referred to the group who have intellectual disabilities and some others who are high functioning or even gifted individuals. You might consider limiting your group to individuals whose intellectual or communication functioning is within a certain range. You should also consider whether having group members with all sorts of different abilities might offer more variety in terms of social experiences for all members of the group.

Here are some other practical suggestions for an autism social skills group:

- Typically, 8–10 members in the group work best.
- Age ranges can vary, but you should hold separate groups for those who are still in school and those who have graduated because the issues faced by each group can be very different.
- Groups tend to work best when members join at the beginning (session 1) and stay until the last group session. This allows members to get comfortable with each other and rely on each other. Allowing members to join after the group has started meeting should be done only in rare circumstances.
- Members should currently be in individual counseling or therapy, or have recently completed individual services. This allows group sessions to focus more on the actual application of social skills rather than spending precious time teaching basic concepts.
- Time-limited groups are recommended (10–12 sessions is an optimal length).

Since group counseling or therapy sessions tend to be time-limited, you want to make the most out of each session. Having a limited amount of time to address issues can be a problem if each session is not focused. Developing a plan for what topics to cover each session allows you to have direction to keep each session focused. You can even develop a manual where you provide outlines and information for each session so that group members can prepare before each session.

You would be wise to look at some of the research on social skills programs. They can provide insight into what topics to include during social skills groups. Mesibov (1984) provided some of the earliest research on social skills groups for adolescents and adults with autism. Laugeson, Frankel, Mogil and Dillon (2009) then later developed the PEERS social skills program, which has been the most researched social skills program for teenagers and young adults with autism.

Laugeson, Frankel, Gantman, Dillon and Mogil (2012) found the PEERS program to be effective for improving social skills and quality of social relationships when at least one parent was involved to help with socialization homework assignments. And then Laugeson, Ellingsen, Sanderson, Tucci and Bates (2014) found that a similar program that incorporated teachers to help with social skills training and exercises was also effective for improving adolescents' social skills and decreasing their social anxiety.

When you look through this research on social skills groups, the following are the main topics that these groups focused on (summarized in Kars et al. 2015):

- Conversational skills
- Trading information
- Two-way conversations
- Electronic communication
- Choosing appropriate friends
- Appropriate use of humor
- Entering a conversation
- Exiting a conversation
- Get-togethers
- Good sportsmanship
- Handling teasing and embarrassing feedback
- Handling bullying and bad reputations
- Handling disagreements
- Rumors and gossip

If you develop a social skills group, use the outline on the following page to focus on each topic in the group. Each week focuses on one main topic in each session.

Social Skills Group Outline

Week	Topic
1.	Conversational skills
2.	Effectively trading information
3.	Handling two-way conversations
4.	Appropriate electronic communication
5.	Choosing appropriate friends
6.	Using humor appropriately
7.	Entering a conversation
8.	Exiting a conversation
9.	Handling get-togethers
10.	Good sportsmanship
11.	Handling teasing and embarrassing feedback
12.	Handling bullying and bad reputations
13.	Handling disagreements
14.	Dealing with rumors and gossip

Although developing your own program does have its benefits in that it is less expensive and you can customize it to fit your clients, there are also benefits to using a pre-developed program.

A pre-developed program can save time and resources since it is completely set up. It will likely cost money up front, but you may end up saving money by not having to take time away from clinical work to develop your program. There is also the added benefit (depending on the program you use) of using a program that has been well-researched.

If you chose to use a pre-developed program, one strong option is the PEERS program, which has been well-researched. PEERS has been shown to be effective for improving social skills and quality of social relationships for teenagers and young adults with autism. Materials for the program are available through the Semele Institute for Neuroscience and Behavior (www.semel.ucla.edu/peers/resources).

Computer-Aided Training

Before moving on from the subject of social skills training, it is useful to consider the subject of computer-aided training. There are several types of programs that provide assistance for social skills training and add (but do not replace) to what is available in individual and group sessions.

Research has shown the following approaches for using computer-aided training to be beneficial for adding to more traditional social skills interventions:

- Video modeling, where the individual is shown videos of how effective social skills should look and then is helped to use those skills (Reichaw & Volmar, 2009). Video cameras, like those on phones and computers, can also help to show the client how they are using these skills and where changes are needed.
- Computer programs focused on helping with facial recognition difficulties (Helt et al. 2008).
- Computerized systems designed to help adolescents with autism learn specific ways to recognize and process the emotions of others (Silver & Oakes, 2001; Ramdoss et al. 2012).
- Virtual reality programs presenting real-life experiences in a safe and controlled manner that allow for unlimited social scenarios replicating different social conditions (Parsons & Mitchell, 2002; Kandalaft, 2013).

You can see that the research on these types of programs goes back to 2002, and that research has shown potential effectiveness for the different types of programs developed since that time. Technology development is occurring at a record pace and so there probably will be much more advanced computer, video and virtual reality programs available when you read this book. But none of the research I summarized here shows any degree of effectiveness separate from a qualified therapist or counselor providing guidance. These programs can be helpful, but only as an adjunct to the work of a qualified and trained professional.

chapter 7
Understanding Friendships

"You don't have enough friends."
"You need more friends."
"You spend too much time by yourself."

These are statements many teenagers and young adults with autism hear from parents and from other well-meaning individuals. The sentiment is usually that the young person needs to spend more time with other people, but the chief concern usually centers around the word *friends* and the (perceived) need to have more of them and do more with them.

But here's the thing: You don't need friends. Friends are nice to have. But they aren't *necessary*. You can survive without them. And if you don't make friends (either by choice or because you don't have the type of interpersonal skills other people are drawn to) you can still survive *and even thrive*.

Many individuals with autism do things primarily by themselves, and in fact, doing things on their own is actually what they prefer. But they are told so often that they *need* to have friends that they doubt themselves. They start to think that there must be something wrong with themselves because they don't feel the need for friends.

This discrepancy between how they prefer to conduct their lives and what their loved ones think they need leads to a lot of arguments. I have probably seen more arguments between parents and teenagers with autism disagreeing about this topic than anything else. And it is not even that addressing the lack of friends would solve all the problems that families see for someone with autism.

Teenagers and young adults without autism are just as likely to have concerns about their family members being too concerned about their friends. I could see a situation where one family could be coming out of my office saying of their child (with autism), "They don't spend enough time with friends," while passing another family coming into my office saying of their child (without autism), "They spend too much time with their friends."

Autism & Friendships

Having an understanding of how teenagers and young adults with autism view friendships can be useful for therapy and counseling. You can use this information to help clients better understand what they are experiencing when it comes to friendships. Helping them see that their views might be different, rather than wrong, can help your clients see themselves in a more favorable light and put less pressure on themselves to change. You might even be able to use this information to help get better communication between your clients and family members.

Adolescents and young adults with autism often differ in what they expect from friends compared to those without autism (Foggo & Webster, 2017). They may have quality relationships with peers, but often prefer more time alone to de-stress and pursue their own interests than do individuals without autism. Bertilsdotter, Brownlow and O'Dell (2015) conducted a large survey of teenagers and adults with autism. They found that while friendships were often cited as important for a good quality of life, the respondents frequently questioned the expectation to have friends and to be sociable.

These authors also found that individuals with autism tended to stress the importance of being alone compared to people without autism. In addition, studies by Jamil, Gragg, and DePape (2017) and Wainer et al. (2013) found that individuals with varying types and degrees of autism showed less interest in, less enjoyment of, and shorter duration of friendships than people without autism.

Adolescents and adults with autism typically define "friendships" as relationships with peers who are kind, trustworthy and someone with whom they can do things they enjoy (Nabors et al. 2017). This is actually not different from what the authors found about what the public at large defined as "friendships."

Also, in a study of 25,185 responses collected via an online news website (none of whom were specifically identified as having autism), Gillespie et al. (2015) found that a large percentage of respondents did not indicate having more than, or much more than, one close friend. They also found that satisfaction with friends was a better predictor of life satisfaction than was number of friends.

So, your clients with autism may want to develop friends but may be more comfortable spending time alone than your clients without autism. And their negative view of themselves or their lives may be more about what they expect they should want (or what their families expect they should) than what they actually want.

Social Relationships: What's the Big Deal?

Emphasizing a need to develop friendships may be an exaggeration of the general importance of social relationships. We may not all need friends, but we do need to interact with people. You need to get along with people at work even if none of them are friends. Heck, you need to get along with people at work even if you don't particularly like them. You also need to be able to interact with people who work at the grocery store, police officers, postal clerks, teachers, government officials and many other people if you want to get important things done. But you do not have to have friendships or even friendly relationships with them. Social interactions are critical for survival, friendships are not.

Let's look at some research on social relationships and their benefits to better understand this relationship. A number of research studies over the past several decades show the benefits of social relationships for lessening the impact of stress. Oxytocin is the neurochemical thought to play a significant role in how social relationships reduce stress, and has been shown to reduce stress in humans and animals (Sullivan & Gunar, 2014).

This neurochemical is involved with the impact of all important social relationships. And, as social relationships help decrease stress (partly by increasing Oxytocin), social isolation tends to increase stress (Detillion et al. 2004; Hennessy, 1986; Vogt, Coe & Levine, 1981).

But these research studies only show that positive social relationships help lessen stress levels. They do not show that any specific type of positive social relationship is needed to decrease these stress levels. Positive social connections serve basic human needs for feeling safe and accepted (Burenk & Dijkstraw, 2012), and that is very likely the reason they help reduce stress levels. But social connections that help with feeling safe and accepted do not have to be friendships. Many types of positive social relationships can accomplish this same outcome.

Emphasizing the importance of human friendships is often couched in a reference to humans as social animals. In a book reviewing comparative social psychology research, Dr. Terry Maple and I (2016) found considerable evidence that being a social animal does not require emotionally intimate relationships like friendships. Having friends is nice and can be beneficial, but it is not necessary for survival in social environments.

Social isolation is detrimental, but there is a huge gap between an individual being socially isolated and having friendships. Could having a large number of generally positive social interactions with other people throughout the day provide the same positive outcomes, in terms of decreased stress levels and decreased feelings of loneliness, as having stronger interactions that could be described as friendships? It is entirely possible. There is nothing in any research on positive social relationships showing that this is not the case.

We know that social relationships are important for human beings. But the extent to which we understand the types of relationships that are important and which aspects of relationships matter is very limited (Reis & Collins, 2004). Perceived loneliness is an important predictor of psychological functioning and morbidity (Cacioppo & Hawkley, 2009). But note that the key word here is perceived. Teenagers and young adults with autism often feel the impact of not having friends (or at least what others would define as "friends") because reactions from others have led to them perceiving themselves as lonely.

In a study of 4,382 typically-developed adults, Demir and Davidson (2013) found that friendships are deemed important for happiness, but even more important are having basic needs met, and feeling competent that one could meet their own needs. Basic need satisfaction and competence satisfaction are much more important for determining happiness than are number of friends or even quality of friendships. Counselors and therapists would do well to take note of this finding.

People tend to be happier if they feel they are competent in doing what they need to do and that they are successfully meeting their basic needs. Helping individuals find a path to feeling this way, regardless of whether they meet others' criteria for a successful social life, can be one very effective way of helping them feel less lonely and more positive about themselves and their lives.

Parents, other family members, teachers, etc., stressing definitive words about what is important (such as friendships and a successful social life) can cause a lot of difficulties for someone because they can sound so absolute (e.g., "You need to have more friends.").

If those words aren't looked at more closely and analyzed for accuracy it can really cause problems for someone who doesn't agree with these words, doesn't live their life according to these words, and may not really understand what the problem is.

How Counselors and Therapists Help

Keep in mind that I am not saying that you, as a counselor or therapist, need to convince your clients that having friends is a bad thing. Social skills training is a large part of what I address throughout this book.

But what I am saying is that you need to help your clients feel more comfortable with where they are at and where they want to be when it comes to friends. They need to make decisions based on what they want and what they think is important, and not on what others tell them is important. And they need to be realistic about what they truly need in their lives versus what would just be nice to have.

One of the reasons I find this so important to address is that, if I am being honest here, many of the clients I work with are just not the type of people who are likely to make friends. Every client I have worked with, both with and without autism, has shown they can interact positively to some degree with other people. But not all of them have shown the ability to make friends. They may just not show the interest level that other people respond to. Or they may just not have a positive style of social interaction that tends to connect with other people.

Also, it may not always be possible to determine why someone does not make friends easily (or at all). Friendships can be complex things to understand. They involve two people (at least), and if one person is not on board then it just doesn't work. I can help a client learn better skills for interacting with people.

But I cannot assure them what the other person's response is going to be. And if the other person is not interested in a friendship, then the social relationship can only go so far.

What we as counselors and therapists need to do is help our clients with autism reach a point where they are satisfied with how they are handling their lives. And if that means that they have a limited numbers of friendships, then that should be fine. If they have to do more things on their own than others do, then so be it. Having a lot of friends can be good, but doing things on your own can be good too. Helping clients get to the point where they are happy with their social relationships is likely to be the point where they feel positive about themselves and their lives.

Cognitive-Behavioral Therapy, Depression & Loneliness

Being alone does not have to mean being lonely.

This is an important rule to stress because it gets to the heart of what lacking friendships often means. Seeing yourself as lacking the social relationships that others tell you that you need (and you may tell yourself that you need) leads to seeing yourself as lonely. And there is quite a bit of research connecting feelings of loneliness and depression (Spithoven et al. 2017; Matthews et al. 2016).

Addressing depression in therapy for someone with autism often involves turning around their negative thinking about themselves and about their lives. Working with someone who feels badly about themselves because of what they don't have socially involves turning around their negative thinking about what that means.

You can help them by teaching them skills they can use to interact more with other people when they need to. But you can also help by lessening their negative feelings about not meeting other people's criteria for what social relationships they should have.

This is the basis of the cognitive-behavioral therapy approach that I often use for someone with autism who also has depression (called comorbid autism and depression). It is an approach that addresses both the cognitive aspects of how the client views himself or herself and the behavioral aspects of how to reach the social goals she or he develops (with a strong focus on these being goals the client sets and not goals other people set).

I usually start this therapy approach by measuring the client's depression. This provides a baseline level for how much depressive symptoms are impacting the person, and allows me to measure progress by using the same instrument at different times during treatment.

Using depressive instruments also lets me see what sorts of negative thinking the person has about themselves and their lives related to feeling lonely and socially isolated.

Depression measures developed for general use among adolescents and adults can be used for adolescents and adults with autism (Gotham, Unruh & Lord, 2015). This includes the Beck Depression Inventory (Beck, Steer & Brown, 1996) and the Adult Self-Report (Achenbach & Rescorla, 2006). For clients who have both autism and intellectual disabilities, the Self-Report Depression Questionnaire (Reynolds & Baker, 1988) would be appropriate.

Once I establish the impact of social difficulties for my client, I then move into a detailed assessment of their social relationships. Basically, I look here at how socially isolated they really are. It may be that they are feeling alone, but actually have more positive social relationships than they realize.

Clients presenting to therapy complaining of few friendships may be downplaying the degree to which they have relationships that could be considered friendships. It may be that they have relationships they do not consider to be friendships but do meet the definition others use.

The following worksheet is one you can use to help your clients determine whether they actually have friends or other types of positive social relationships. It is a worksheet designed specifically to gauge your client's definition of what makes someone their friend, and to get an accurate view (from your client's perspective) about their social relationships.

Defining Friendships

Client Name: _____

What do you mean when you call someone your friend? (Ex. kind person, trustworthy, can do fun things with, etc.)

Client's Response: _____

_____

_____

Do you have anyone you consider to be a friend?   Yes   No

If yes, what are their names? _____

_____

_____

What do you enjoy doing with them? _____

_____

_____

Do you have anyone you consider to be close to being a friend?   Yes   No

If yes, what are their names? _____

_____

_____

What do you enjoy doing with them? _____

_____

_____

One question that may come up when completing this form is, Do online friends count? And the answer here is It depends. If they mean friends on a social media site (e.g., Facebook), those probably do not count. Individuals with whom your client communicates with regularly online or plays games with only on a regular basis could definitely be considered friends. Typically, the rule would be that the individual has to meet at least one of the criteria they set (on the form) for the definition of friend.

What is particularly useful to keep in mind here is that there is absolutely no consistent research showing that friendships made through social networking are any better or worse than friendships made other ways. They can be as close and also as fulfilling as other friendships.

Friendships made through social networking can provide benefits for individuals who feel isolated, like teenagers and young adults with autism. But there is a need for young people to be careful of who they accept as friends online and how they manage their online social networks (Best, Taylor & Manktelow, 2015; Best, Manktelow & Taylor, 2014). I find that the definition of friends used in the previous worksheet helps the client gauge whether any of the criteria he or she set themselves are met with their online social relationships.

Once I establish an accurate picture of my client's social circle, I then move into discussing the degree to which lacking social relationships is causing difficulties for my client. I am specifically trying to gauge whether the client is making realistic judgments or whether they actually need more social relationships.

This again gets to the point of addressing whether clients are basing their negative thinking on their own interpretation about their lives or whether they are basing their interpretation on what other people say they should have in their lives.

Basically what I am looking at here is: "Who is telling you that you need more friends or more social relationships?" and, "Where are you getting the impression that having more social relationships is absolutely necessary?"

This can be a tricky subject to address because the expectation that someone needs a lot of friends to be satisfied with their lives can be pretty strongly ingrained.

So I take steps to make sure to ask these questions in ways that do not seem judgmental. I am very careful to make sure that I am not asking it in a way that sounds like I am challenging the views that the person comes in with. At this point (e.g., the beginning of treatment) I am just asking a question. I may very well want to challenge those views later, but if I sound too challenging at first this could very well damage the therapeutic rapport.

Keep in mind that one of the reasons why being very careful about challenging client's expectations up front is so important is because those expectations may very well be coming from parents.

Parents are often the ones who are prompting teenagers or young adults to get into therapy because they are concerned about them not having enough friends. They may very well look around at their child's peers and see that they have many more friendships and social interactions than their child. They are concerned about their child based on their impression that she or he does not have what seems to make other people happy.

So, early comments about friendships and social expectations should not directly challenge a client's views of friendships (that may have to be done, but is better to address after a solid therapeutic relationship is established). The comments should not challenge the parents' social expectations. However, these comments should spell out expectations for how friendship issues might be addressed. Here are two sample statements (one for clients and one for parents) that I find helpful for addressing these issues:

For Clients: "I know that you came in here concerned about friendships. And we are definitely going to work on that. I just want to make sure that you recognize that simply having more friends is not what is going to help you feel better. It is not as if having no friends always makes people sad and having a hundred friends always makes them happy. What is important is that you are satisfied with the social relationships you have. Making you satisfied with your life is what we are going to work on. OK?"

For Parents: "I know that you came in here concerned about your son's/daughter's friendships. And we are definitely going to work on that. I just want to make sure you understand that simply making more friends is not necessarily going to be what helps your son/daughter. I think we can all agree that there is no truth to the statement: Having no friends always makes people miserable and having a hundred friends always makes people happy. What matters is having quality social relationships that help your child feel positive about themselves. And helping your child feel positive about themselves and their relationships is what I am going to focus on. OK?"

Here are some of the topics I cover with the new client in cognitive-behavior therapy focused on concerns with friendships:

- Establish specifically why and how the client thinks friendships are a problem (e.g., too few friends, keeps losing friends, does not do much with friends).
- If parents/family members are involved, address whether there is agreement about friendship issues—that is, are the parents seeing the problem differently than the client?
- Determine how the client defines friends and how many friends (fitting in with their definition) they actually have.
- Assess the impact that friendship issues have on the client's functioning (usually using some type of depression measure).
- Clarify why the client thinks friendship problems are an issue that needs to be addressed.

What all this allows me to do is to gauge the negative thinking contributing to my client's feelings of loneliness and to their depressive symptoms. I use all this information to get a clear picture of the specific types of negative thoughts the person is having and how they may be contributing to an unrealistic view of his or her life. And then later, I will address these types of negative thoughts using cognitive-therapy approaches.

Anderson and Morris (2006) laid out some suggestions for cognitive therapy for teenagers and young adults with autism that I have found useful in my own practice. They utilize the following specific approaches during cognitive therapy:

- Provide affective education (teaching relationship between negative thinking and mood)
- Address unrealistic negative thinking (e.g., "I need a lot of friends to be happy")
- Create alternative, realistic self-statements
- Monitor negative thinking (typically using some form of Thought Record, which are journals clients use to keep track of specific thoughts

in problem situations) and then monitor the use of alternative realistic self-statements

They also recommend a therapy approach that does not emphasize rational arguments since the rigid thinking associated with autism often makes any sort of arguments difficult. They emphasize instead a focus on more realistic, concrete self-statements to replace the more negative self-statements associated with feeling lonely and depressed.

When addressing friendship issues in autism, the type of negative and unrealistic thinking involved is usually the all or none type. This is a type of negative thinking associated with depressed mood where the person thinks "I must have all of something," or "I must have none of something." In the case of friendships, the thinking would often be: "I must be happy if I have a lot of friends," or "I must be unhappy if I have no (or only a few) friends." This clearly is an unrealistic dichotomy many people would disagree with, and which the research shows is not accurate.

Taking Anderson and Morris' recommendation into account, I find the best approach to addressing this type of negative thinking (or similar types of negative thinking) would not be to confront it with a discussion (or "rational argument") of how it is inaccurate. That would be an approach you might take with some clients when using cognitive therapy, but it does not tend to be effective for helping someone with autism.

What is more effective is developing specific positive and realistic self-statements that counter the more negative self-statements. One example might be: "I do not need a lot of friends to be happy" or "I can be happy with the number of friends that I have."

Once I address the alternative types of self-statements that could help my client, (such as "It is OK to do things alone"), then I may want to help the client to see the truth of those statements. So, for example, if I think the person will find it helpful, I might bring up the research and literature reviews I cited earlier that concluded that friendships are not necessary for survival. I don't bring this up as arguments but, rather, as alternative viewpoints that help support the self-statements that I am suggesting are accurate ones.

I also provide opportunities for the person to experience the accuracy of the self-statements we discuss. One specific self-statement I address often is: "It is OK to do things alone." Very often the negative thinking related to needing friends is accompanied by the equally negative thinking of "It is always a bad thing for me to do things on my own." This is not just the case for people with autism. People often suffer from a very negative view of what it means to do things by themselves. There is no logical reason for this point of view and it is often the case that people can enjoy themselves very much doing things by themselves. It is just that they need to give themselves permission to do things without having someone else along.

On the next page is a worksheet that you can give to your client to help address unrealistic thinking about doing things alone. It is called I Like Me as a reflection of the positives that can be attached to a person enjoying their own company. I find it useful as an accompaniment for addressing clients' unrealistic and negative thinking about having to do things by themselves.

I Like Me

What do you like about yourself?

_____

_____

_____

What do you like to do for fun (even if no one else is with you)?

_____

_____

_____

What are some other things you could do by yourself?

_____

_____

_____

Do you think you are a good person? What makes you a good person?

_____

_____

_____

Do you think you are an interesting person? What makes you an interesting person?

_____

_____

_____

Cognitive-behavior therapy continues beyond this point focused on increasing the use of more positive and realistic self-statements to help replace the negative self-statements associated with feeling lonely and depressed.

Using the Thought Record on an ongoing basis helps to increase the use of the more positive self-statements, and providing homework assignments can help to reinforce how strongly the client holds to the alternative self-statements and alternative ways of thinking about social relationships.

Once I have worked with a client to develop a more realistic and positive view of friendships and social relationships I then work with them on developing more realistic social goals. When a client with autism develops a more realistic view of things like "What is a friend?" "How important are friendships?" and "Can I be more comfortable being on my own?" I think they are then better able to develop appropriate and meaningful goals for addressing their social network.

chapter 8

Anger Management

Let me tell you about Roger. He is a young man who was diagnosed with autism as a young child and received specialized services for much of his life. He has problems with social skills, communication and perseveration that have impacted his functioning almost every day of his life. In school he had many behavior problems and spent a good deal of time in the principal's office.

But Roger always had a good work ethic. He did his homework even when he found it difficult. He put effort into his assignments and always turned them in. He kept his grades up even when his behavior difficulties were causing him problems. He did pretty good academically and graduated with slightly above average grades.

Once graduated, Roger was able to get a job at a large store where he stocked shelves. It was one of many stores owned by a large company. Working for a large company was an advantage for Roger because the policies of where to stock items were set by company headquarters. He did not have to debate with managers or co-workers about where items went because that policy had already been set elsewhere. And he always worked the overnight shift so his need to interact with other people was limited.

Roger did very well at that job until he had a disagreement with a co-worker. He did not usually have to interact much with other employees but sometimes it was part of the job. On one occasion a co-worker criticized how long it took Roger to do something. Roger let that employee have it. He yelled and screamed for several minutes, walked away, and then yelled and screamed at the co-worker again several minutes later. He kept that up several times throughout his shift, and then picked it back up again during the next shift. He perseverated so much on his anger about being treated badly by this co-worker, or what he perceived as being treated badly by the co-worker, that his behaviors eventually led to his being fired.

Roger then obtained another job at a similar large store where he once again worked stocking shelves overnight. And he did well again at that job until he befriended a female co-worker and another co-worker made fun of how much interest he showed in her.

It was true that Roger probably spent too much time trying to talk with the female co-worker and made too evident his strong romantic interest in her. But this other co-worker was equally relentless in how often he made fun of Roger, and after a few weeks of this, Roger reached his breaking point. He again yelled and screamed multiple times at the co-worker and this time made threats about stabbing him. This ended up getting Roger fired again.

This example shows the types of problems someone like Roger often runs into with anger. It was not that the situations making Roger angry were unusual. One involved him getting angry about being criticized and one involved him getting angry about being made fun of. Both are, I would argue, situations that would make anyone angry.

It was not that the situations made him angry that caused problems for Roger. It was how he responded. His yelling and screaming, along with his perseveration, led to him not only being disruptive, but also to him not being able to focus on anything related to his job.

We all get angry. But it is how we react to that anger that matters. Individuals with autism already have problems with social skills. But when you add anger to the mix, that is where the difficulties become even more intense. Being irritated or bothered by how someone acts takes on a look of hatred (rather than irritation) because of how that anger exhibits itself.

Anger management problems typically arise because of how others react to angry behaviors. Teenagers and adults who start yelling, screaming and hitting things cause other people to worry that the person is losing it. Questions like "What can we do to keep them to stop?" and "Are they going to start hitting me, or their brother or sister, after they stop hitting the wall?" are examples of questions people ask when someone seems to lose control over anger.

These types of problems often lead parents, teachers or others who are worried about a teenager or young adult to suggest, or even insist, that he or she get counseling. In fact, aggression and irritability are some of the most common reasons why teenagers and young adults receive therapy and counseling (Sukhodolsky et al. 2016). This is no less the case with autism than it is for other teenagers and young adults.

As much as angry behaviors in a person with autism may cause concern for others, they can also cause intense problems for the person themselves. This was certainly the case with Roger, who not only became increasingly angry at what he saw as being treated unfairly, but also increasingly worried that he would not be able to effectively control that anger. He got caught up in a vicious cycle. As he became more anxious about not being able to control his anger, he escalated his behaviors in an attempt to exert control over the situation, which in turn increased his anxiety.

To an outsider, it appeared that he was giving little consideration to how his anger impacted other people. He would yell louder and louder, be more threatening with his behaviors, and show less and less evidence that he was worried if his behaviors bothered anyone.

This is often a problem for teenagers and young adults with autism. This sort of troubling response becoming more and more disruptive or aggressive in ways that show less and less concern about other people, often caused difficulties when teenagers and young adults deal with anger.

Autism & Empathy Issues

What we know from the research on autism is that people with autism do not care less about other people. They may, however, look like they care less about other people. In a study of adults with autism (ages ranging from 19 to 60 years old), Smith (2009) found that his subjects were not lacking in emotional and empathic feelings but, rather, had difficulty in showing these feelings.

This study result coincides with brain research showing that emotional empathy, associated with the left anterior insula section of the brain, is not impaired in persons with autism.

Another misunderstanding is that people with autism are "antisocial" (thus making angry moments particularly scary). But this is not accurate. People who are truly antisocial lack concern and care for other people, while those with autism simply look like they don't care.

There is considerable research showing that the lack of social connectedness and poor social behaviors found in autism have completely different causes and symptoms from what occurs in antisocial behaviors. Autism presents with social problems and difficulties with social connectedness that are associated with specific types of atypical brain activity.

Similar problems may be present in aggressive personality disorders and psychopathy, but the atypical brain activity is not the same as what is associated with autism (Bird et al. 2010).

Here is a summary of research findings showing clear differences between autism and antisocial disorders. You might find it useful when discussing autism with people who mistake a lack of social connectedness with a lack of emotional and empathic connectedness.

- Although autism and antisocial disorders share impaired social functioning as hallmark characteristics, they show distinction in their genetic, cognitive and neural profiles (Blair, 2008).
- Autism is associated with impairments in reasoning about the mental status of others whereas antisocial disorders difficulties are related to the processing of emotional stimuli, fear conditioning and moral reasoning (Anckarsäter, 2006).
- With autism there is an inability to demonstrate caring about others, rather than a lack of ability to do so, that is found in antisocial disorders.

The bottom line is that neurological issues associated with antisocial behaviors are not the same as neurological issues in autism (Raine, 2002).

Having established the separateness of these disorders, it's important to note that though they are not the same, they are not mutually exclusive. An individual with autism does not necessarily have antisocial traits but may have both autistic and antisocial traits.

Fitzgerald (2015) used the term Criminal Autistic Psychopathy to describe the co-occurrence of these sets of traits. He did not specify how often this occurs, but he did describe it as occurring in a small number of persons with autism.

Your client's age will affect their observable emotions and behaviors. Using neurological evidence, Wallace et al. (2012) found that emotional response and the ability to show empathy becomes more difficult as individuals with autism get older. Blakemore (2010) found increased problems in teenagers and young adults with autism. Modifying their behaviors to reflect that they care about others and that they are trying to understand how others feel emotionally decreased those problems.

Likelihood of Anger

We have some insight into which type of client is most likely to have anger issues. Mazurek, Kanne and Wodka (2013) found that symptom severity, including self-injurious behavior, ritualistic behavior, and resistance to change all served as predictors of aggression in adolescents with autism.

That said, individuals with autism can have difficulty handling anger simply due to their decreased executive functioning skills, which in turn increases disinhibition and impulsivity. You will want to note that these symptoms tend to increase as the severity of autistic symptoms increase.

Therapeutic Approaches

Using behavioral strategies to help improve how individuals with autism handle anger and how they think through dealing with anger can be effective for decreasing anger management problems (Sofronoff et al. 2007). This is because these interventions help individuals with autism learn better skills for handling emotions and interacting with others. Interventions also help to decrease impulsiveness as the individual thinks through how to better handle problem situations.

Most effective behavioral strategies for anger management and aggressive behaviors in autism fall into one of three groups: antecedent strategies and contingency management strategies. All three approaches produce good results in treating aggressiveness (Brosnan, 2011).

Antecedent manipulation strategies include prompting, photographic activity schedules, interpersonal requests and choice making. Reinforcement strategies include functional communication training, differential reinforcement procedures, noncontingent attention and differential negative reinforcement. Consequence manipulation includes extinction, overcorrection, response cost and time out.

Following is a summary of these behavioral strategies and definitions along with advice on how they are applied differently for individuals considered lower functioning versus those considered higher functioning.

Behavioral Interventions for Addressing Anger

Antecedent Strategies

Prompting

In this approach, you physically or verbally direct the person to engage in behaviors that will help lessen problems with anger. For lower-functioning individuals, physical prompting might involve moving them to a different area as a way to get them to "walk away" from a potentially anger-inducing situation. *Higher-functioning individuals, will be verbally told to "walk away" from the problem situation.*

Photograph Activity Schedules (Picture Schedules):

In this technique, we use visual prompts such as small pictures, photos or words on a card or in a small notebook to spell out a sequence of steps for the individual to perform in a given situation. *For children, the schedules lay out simple social skills, dressing and grooming steps, and basic behaviors. For adults, picture schedules are often used for job training, completing tasks in an independent-living regime and more generally for setting up a schedule.*

For anger management, you could create a card with pictures of the different ways to deal effectively with problem situations. This intervention is based on the research findings that individuals with autism tend to learn better when visual prompts are used. Use concrete images (photos) for lower-functioning individuals. Higher-functioning individuals may find a written list of tasks to be easy to follow. You will want to combine verbal instruction with the schedule, making the instruction as concrete as possible.

Interpersonal Requests

This involves the development of "scripts" to use with others. For anger management, they are used to help the individual make effective requests of others with the goal being to reduce the likelihood of an angry situation. As with scripts for social skills training, you want the complexity and detail of the steps to match the person's functional ability.

Choice Making

Here you would walk the individual through a series of "if-then" statements about how best to make choices in the situations that they will be encountering. When working with anger management, you can ask the question, "How do you know when you are starting to get angry?" The client's responses—their statements about feeling angry—can then be used as the prompts for discussing successive sets of decisions. The outcome is that they will learn the steps to take to make better choices.

Reinforcement-Based Strategies

Functional Communication Training

In this method, you train clients to use effective communication—rather than resort to angry behaviors—to get what they need. With lower-functioning individuals you want to focus on specific statements they can use for getting what they want, and with higher-functioning individuals you work on specific strategies they can use to express their wants and needs more effectively.

Differential Reinforcement Procedures

This method goes hand-in-hand with functional communication training but is also part of some of the antecedent strategies. The idea is for your client to earn a desired reinforcer (reward) for using more effective behaviors when dealing with situations that cause them anger. To avoid angry behaviors such as yelling and screaming you can make use of tangible rewards, like games or specific food items, but can also use nontangible reinforcers, like attention and positive praise.

Noncontingent Attention

In this method you develop a schedule where the client receives attention regardless of what behaviors they are doing at the time. What this creates is the opportunity for your client to learn that he or she can get the attention she or he wants without having to rely on problematic behaviors. This is particularly helpful for situations like one where a client is using yelling or screaming as a way of getting attention. You could develop the schedule for use in any setting, including the therapy session itself.

Differential Negative Reinforcement

This is a method in which the reward is the removal of something negative (such as an irritant). It is different from the other differential reinforcement procedures in that it involves the removal of a stimuli as opposed to the presentation of a stimuli for appropriate behaviors. Here's an example of how this can be used in anger management. A teenager throws a tantrum to get out of the classroom, but is only allowed to leave once they communicate effectively how they are feeling and what they want.

<u>Consequence Manipulation Strategies</u>

Extinction

This approach is sometimes called ignoring, and by this we mean ignoring in a very strategic way. It is based on the view that the best way to change a behavior is not by giving it positive or negative attention, but by giving it NO attention. People look to get attention for their behaviors. If they cannot get positive attention, they will take negative attention. *With extinction you create a plan in which the people around your client give no attention to the problem behaviors associated with anger.* This approach is most effective when combined with differential reinforcement of alternative anger management behaviors.

Overcorrection

In this approach, your clients have to do more than is fair to pay for problems they caused because of their angry behaviors. If, for example, your client breaks a dish on the floor when angry, their consequence would be not just to clean up the dish, but to clean up the whole kitchen. This step helps increase the individual's motivation for using more effective behaviors in the future.

Response Cost

With this approach, clients lose reinforcers (rewards) when they exhibit problem behaviors. It is most clearly associated with token economy systems where the individual has to give back a certain number of tokens when they exhibit target problem behaviors. It can be used for things like computer time, where time might be deducted from time allowed on the computer whenever the individual shows problem anger management behaviors.

Time Out

This is probably the most common behavioral approach for addressing problem behaviors with younger children. When given a time out, the individual sits alone and does nothing. It can be adapted for teens, as well. With teenagers, you can use it as a teaching opportunity for how they might respond to anger on their own. You want to help them get to the point in which they give themselves a time out before they start to have problems with angry behaviors.

These approaches work well together and can be effectively combined to produce a comprehensive anger management treatment program for your client. You will want to consider working with parents and teachers to develop a behavioral plan that lays out when and how prompting and reinforcement is to be used. This will increase the consistency of support for your client's anger management training. During sessions, you can both train your client to use more effective skills for handling anger and initiate the reinforcement approaches that were decided upon.

Working with Anger

It is important that your client recognizes the first signs of anger rising. To make that happen, you can use the worksheet, What Anger Feels Like, to help them see clearly what anger feels like, and also to increase the consistency with which they recognize themselves having problems with anger.

What Anger Feels Like

Tell me about two situations within the past two weeks where you felt angry.

Name: _____

Situation 1
What made you angry about what was going on?

_____

_____

Think about that situation. How did you know you were angry? How did it feel? (be specific)

_____

_____

Situation 2
What made you angry about what was going on?

_____

_____

Think about that situation. How did you know you were angry? How did it feel? (be specific)

_____

_____

Tell me some other ways that your body feels when you are angry.

_____

Tell me some other things you are thinking when you are angry.

_____

Mindfulness and Autism

Singh et al. (2011) found mindfulness to be an effective way to help adolescents with autism decrease their use of physical aggression when dealing with anger. Singh taught the adolescents to quickly shift the focus of their attention (away from the anger-provoking thoughts or events) to a neutral place on their body—usually the soles of their feet. I have outlined the basic steps of Singh's approach below to give you an idea of his process, but what is presented here is just a single example of a mindfulness approach that can be used.

Mindfulness as a therapeutic tool is prominent throughout the counseling and therapy fields and most professionals seem to have their own preferred approach, so you will need to determine how to incorporate his process into your own. (By the way, in the study, the teens were taught to do mindfulness by their parents.) Here is Singh's process:

- The adolescents are told to sit comfortably in a soft chair, with feet flat on the floor and hands resting on their laps. They then close their eyes to increase concentration and narrow their focus to the present moment.
- Their parents then read a script instructing them to shift their attention from the anger to a neutral object. This is done in a calm and soft voice.
- This practice did not require the presence of any trigger for their aggressive behavior, but they were encouraged to use the procedure whenever they felt themselves becoming increasingly angry.
- Each adolescent was required to practice the technique at least twice a day on their own or with their parents. They were also told to use the attention-shifting technique whenever an incident occurred that got them angry enough that it could elicit aggressive behavior.
- Once they had learned the basics of the mindfulness procedure they were given an audiotape of the instructions that they could use to practice on their own.
- This training was ended when each adolescent did not engage in physically aggressive behaviors for four consecutive weeks.

This is an approach that, in my experience, teenage and young adults find both useful and interesting. Just to clarify a little more (and show why it can be interesting) the "neutral object" that I refer to here were the soles of a subject's feet. So, when someone was told to focus on a "neutral object," they were being told to focus on his or her feet. Here are the actual instructions that were included in the Singh article:

- Now, shift all your attention fully to the soles of your feet.
- Slowly, move your toes, feel your shoes covering your feet, feel the texture of your socks, the curve of your arch, and the heels of your feet against the back of your shoes. If you do not have shoes on, feel the floor or carpet with the soles of your feet.

One other thing to keep in mind is that there is no evidence that the main approaches used for teaching mindfulness to teenagers and young adult clients are any less effective for helping clients with autism.

Cognitive Reappraisal

Another viable therapy approach is cognitive reappraisal, which Samson et al. (2015) found that to be helpful for adolescents with autism dealing with anger. This method is a cognitive therapy approach where the individual—in the moment—replaces negative thinking with neutral or positive thoughts. In effect, they create alternative thought patterns to lessen the impact of an emotional situation.

Take, for example, the person who gets upset whenever they are running late. They may focus on thoughts such as, "People will get angry at me if I am late," which can increase their anger and anxiety. With cognitive reappraisal, they might instead ask themselves: "How likely is it really that someone will be very angry at me if I am 15 minutes late?" Using a series of questions like this could eventually get them to the point where the individual says to themselves (and means it): "People really won't be bothered very much if I am 15 minutes late."

What the Samson study found was that the adolescents with autism could benefit from cognitive reappraisal: Those individuals with autism often needed more help developing the cognitive appraisals possibly due to difficulties comprehending how different types of thinking impact social behaviors, but were able to use the appraisals effectively once developed. Clients with autism in this study were not as effective as others with drawing conclusions on their own that they needed for developing reappraisals.

But there was evidence that once they had the reappraisals they were able to use them effectively. What you have here is evidence, as has been the case elsewhere in this book, that providing specific statements your clients can use when faced with emotionally upsetting situations can help to lessen the impact of difficult situations (in this case situations where your clients are angry). You may find it helpful to address anger by giving the reappraisal statement to the client on your own (e.g., telling them to repeat: "People won't be upset if I am a few minutes late") without necessarily needing them to come up with specific conclusions themselves. You may need to spend more time in session helping to provide support for the validity of the reappraisal statements than you would for other clients (since the client may not have deduced the statement on his or her own), but the statements can still be very effective.

On the following page is a list of different cognitive reappraisal statements that your clients might find useful for handling anger. They are specifically related to situations where negative thinking is likely to be related to anger difficulties. You can encourage your clients to use these short, concrete and direct statements as steps they use in terms of saying things to themselves (self-statements) for lessening problems with anger.

Cognitive Reappraisal Statements for Anger

"I'm allowed to feel angry. I just can't yell at (or hit) people."

"People do like having me around."

"It is OK if I am a little late."

"No one is going to yell at me for being late."

"I will be alright even if things are a little different today."

"My family loves me even when I get upset."

"Not everyone has to agree with me."

"I am a good person even when people disagree with me."

"My schedule can change without it being a big deal."

"Life is not always fair and that is OK."

"People like me even if they disagree with me."

"It is good to smile even if people do not smile back."

Relaxation training is also an effective approach for improving anger management. Learning how to relax has been shown to help clients in many different anger management programs and has been specifically shown to help clients with intellectual, developmental and mental health problems (Koslowski et al. 2016).

Progressive muscle relaxation is one of the most effective approaches for learning how to relax. The process for helping your clients learn this approach to anger management skills is outlined on the following page.

Progressive Muscle Relaxation

Learning how to relax can be helpful for dealing with anxiety and can also be helpful for dealing with anger. If you learn how to relax then you can use these steps to help yourself calm down when you are angry. In this exercise you will learn to bring about relaxation throughout your body by learning how to relax several different parts of your body.

Tense and relax different muscle groups. As you focus on each area, breathe in deeply, hold for a few seconds, then release slowly for a few seconds. Repeat each area three times before moving on to the next area.

Face

- Scrunch up and then release

Arms and Shoulders

- Stretch arms out in front

- Raise arms as high as possible

- Drop arms & hang them loose

Hands

- Imagine squeezing an orange as hard as possible

- Then imagine dropping it on the floor

- Let arm & hand go limp

- Switch to the other arm

Stomach

- Clench stomach muscles briefly

- release and relax

Legs and Feet

- Press toes hard against the floor

- Release & relax

Here is a final note regarding anger management. Rumination (also known as perseveration) is a significant problem associated with autism, and research has shown that anger rumination is one of the most common types (Patel et al. 2017).

Teenagers and young adults often focus repetitively on specific situations and topics that make them angry. Addressing this can be very difficult as it is not the type of behavior that responds very well to approaches used to address anger management skills effectively. In the next chapter we will look at some approaches that can be effective for perseveration.

chapter 9

Perseveration and Stereotyped Behaviors

Perseverative and stereotyped behaviors are disruptive behaviors that can really make someone with autism stand out. When you hear people describe someone with autism as strange or weird, chances are it is these behaviors they are referring to. They are, unfortunately, very, very difficult to get under any sort of control.

Perseveration is repetitive verbal behavior that includes repeating certain phrases (e.g., repeating lines from movies) and repeating statements focused on very limited topics (e.g., talking constantly about trains). These behaviors are frequently disruptive and very difficult to redirect (Attwood, 1997).

Stereotypy, also known as self-stimulatory behaviors, are repetitive physical movements. They include repetitive body movements (e.g., rocking, scratching and arm-flapping), as well as repetitively moving an object—usually by moving it with their hands (e.g., flicking fingers at an object, pounding an object on the table, and winding string around things).

These not only disrupt activities in progress and annoy people, but also impact the person's physical functioning. A person focused on repetitively moving an object will find it difficult to perform a functional task since both the hands and the mind are engaged with the stereotypy.

Coping Skills & Perseveration

Understanding and treating perseverative behaviors is not a one size fits all sort of endeavor. There is not one single approach that is going to work with every teenager or young adult with this sort of problem.

Having said that, it is interesting that research pretty consistently shows that improving coping skills is what helps reduce perseverative behaviors (Williams, Siegel & Mazefsky, 2017). If you help your client cope better with whatever is contributing to the perseveration then you have a good chance of reducing those behaviors. But then you have the question, "Cope with what?"

When you look at the different approaches to treating perseverative behaviors, you see that they are all ways of coping with something. It may be coping with a need for stimulation. Or it may be coping with anxiety, anger or excitement. We all have to cope with something and oftentimes teenagers and young adults with autism cope by using repetitive behaviors.

Before moving on here, it is worth mentioning that exactly why these specific behaviors occur repetitively is not certain. There's something neurological about it and it seems that the repetitive behaviors have a sort of soothing effect. People need to be soothed in a lot of different situations, and for people with autism it's these repetitive behaviors that seem to do the trick. Finding other ways of getting the same type of soothing without relying on disruptive behaviors is really at the heart of what all these interventions try to do.

Coping with a Need for Stimulation

Repetitive behaviors in autism are often reinforced by the stimulation they create (Berkson, 1983; Lovaas, Newson & Hickman, 1987). A teenager with autism, for example, might repeat a phrase from a movie because of the auditory stimulation that it produces. And arm-flapping, a common self-stimulatory behavior, often produces a great deal of physical stimulation.

It is not that the person purposely looks for stimulation, but it is still the stimulation, that reinforces the behaviors. Because of this, it is often possible to find some less disruptive behavior that can help to decrease the more disruptive behaviors.

Here are some steps to consider when addressing replacement behaviors for more disruptive behaviors:

- Identify the specific behavior to be addressed.
- Observe the behaviors in a number of different situations (if possible).

- Try to identify some specific sort of stimulation that seems to reinforce the behavior. Keep in mind that it is unnecessary to identify "why" that stimulation might reinforce the behavior.
- Try to design some sort of less intrusive and less disruptive behavior that could produce the same stimulation.
- Present that alternative behavior to your client and suggest they try using it.
- Measure effectiveness of this behavior for reducing more disruptive behaviors (using weekly assignments and data collection in between sessions).

Coping with Stress

Stress is one other factor contributing to repetitive behaviors (Joyce, Honey, Leekam, Barrett & Rodgers, 2017). Someone with autism may be engaging in repetitive behaviors because they help to reduce their feelings of anxiety and stress.

What all this means is that your client may be using repetitive behaviors to reduce stress but may not actually be aware that this is the reason. So if you ask him or her, "Why do you keep flapping your arms?" or "Why do you keep saying the same thing over and over?" your client very likely cannot give you a reason. He or she may acknowledge "doing it makes me feel better" (or, more likely, "I feel worse if I don't do it"), but would not likely verbalize they are stressed or anxious before engaging in these behaviors.

Having limited awareness of anxiety's role in repetitive behaviors limits how likely typical stress management (e.g., relaxation) exercises are going to be in treating these behaviors. In the chapter on anger management, I noted that relaxation management strategies are as effective for someone with autism as they are for someone without autism.

One limitation here is that using these strategies often requires that the person recognize they are anxious or upset. But with repetitive behaviors, your client may not always recognize stress, anxiety or emotional distress being what they experience before these behaviors.

Physical exercise is one type of stress management that has been found to reduce repetitive behaviors. This can be particularly useful for repetitive behaviors in autism because teenagers and young adults are often told exercise is good for you even if they aren't told specific reasons why (in this case, that it leads to less stress and, as a result, less repetitive behaviors).

Kern, Koegel and Dunlap (1984) showed that different types of physical exercise had an impact on arm-flapping behaviors for individuals with autism. Physical exercise was found to produce the same level of stress reduction and physical stimulation as the repetitive behaviors.

These authors found that 15 minutes of mild exercise tended to have little effect on repetitive behaviors (arm-flapping in this example), but that 15 minutes of vigorous exercise consistently did have an effect on reducing its severity and duration.

Using vigorous exercise tended to be less disruptive than the arm-flapping behavior in large part because it did not stand out so much (as people would tend to see the behavior and say, "Oh, that person is exercising," rather than say, "Why is that weird person flapping their arms so much?").

This research showed that exercise was a way of decreasing the repetitive behaviors, although the exact reason why it worked was not clearly identified. Given that exercise is often used as a way of decreasing stress, and given that stress is one factor associated with repetitive behaviors, you could reasonably conclude that stress management was one reason why it worked.

Coping with Anger

Perseverative statements are also often associated with increased anger (Patel et al. 2017). These are often put in the category of "ruminative thoughts," indicating that the individual is perseverating on angry topics and verbalizing them.

Research has shown a relationship between anger and perseverative statements, although there is limited research on effective treatment for addressing this particular problem. There was one small study (Spek et al. 2013) showing that the type of mindfulness exercise I described in the last chapter could be effective for helping to decrease perseverative behaviors when they are associated with anger.

Perseveration as Reinforcement

When therapists and counselors talk about perseverative behaviors and other repetitive behaviors in autism, it is usually in the context of trying to reduce them. And this is important given how disruptive these behaviors can be. However, perseverative and self-stimulatory behaviors also have physical reinforcement qualities that can be used to help reinforce more desired behaviors.

Koegel et al. (2012) and Baker et al. (1998) focused on improving social involvement of teens with autism by having them get involved with groups related to their perseverative interests. The strategy worked to increase the teens' social involvement, and there was no evidence that this caused increased perseverative behaviors outside of the group meetings.

As an individual works within session to decrease their repetitive behaviors, they will find it relaxing and reinforcing to be given some free time to perseverate. You will also find that this perseveration break aids in reinforcing the new, appropriate behavior.

Several studies have shown that rewarding an individual for correct responses of behaviors with time to engage in perseverative behaviors is effective. This is true for getting the individual to provide correct verbal responses (Wolery, Kirk & Gast, 1985); to increase the use of appropriate sentences (Hung, 1978); and to decrease aggressive behaviors (Charlop-Christy & Haymes, 1996). Lang et al. (2011) also found that including the perseverative topics of interest (e.g., trains, vacuum cleaners, and so on) within the treatment sessions helped improve the effectiveness of cognitive-behavioral therapy.

Using perseveration as a reinforcement for more positive social behaviors may seem counterproductive. But it does have the potential benefit of helping to decrease the negative impact of perseverative behaviors by increasing the client's use of more appropriate social behaviors.

If, for example, you can get your client to practice in session using more positive social behaviors (by reinforcing their use of these behaviors with allowing them time to perseverate without interruption), then you may help to lessen the impact of the perseveration in their social world. If your client is using more appropriate social behaviors when interacting with peers then their perseveration might stand out less.

Steps for Decreasing Behavior Problems

Allowing clients uninterrupted time to perseverate has also been used as a means for helping individuals learn ways of controlling their perseverations.

A good technique to help with this is the Red Card, Green Card Exercise (or the Red Card, Green Card Game for younger children).

This exercise rewards an individual for successfully engaging in non-perseverative topics for specific time periods in exchange for being allowed to perseverate for specific time periods.

Here is the method for the Red Card, Green Card Game that Salisbury (2015) found effective for decreasing the frequency and duration of a teenager's stereotyped behaviors:

- Two cards were used, one red and one green.
- Each card was held up for five-minute periods.
- When the red card was held up, the experimenter said, "Red card: quiet mouth and hands down."
- For any subsequent episode of stereotypy, the red card was shown to the participant again and the experimenter repeated, "Red card: quiet mouth and hands down."
- When the green card was held up, the experimenter said, "Green card (student name)." When green card was up, the students were allowed to engage in stereotyped behaviors without being interrupted.

Similar steps were used by Fisher, Rodriguez and Own (2013) to help decrease the verbal perseverations of a teenage male diagnosed with an autism spectrum disorder. This approach would be more effective for a teenager or young adult who is considered to be higher functioning (more the Red Card, Green Card Exercise than the Red Card, Green Card Game):

- The therapist held up a card that was either green or red.
- When the card was green, the adolescent was allowed to talk about whatever he wanted.
- When the card was red, the therapist would ignore the adolescent whenever he engaged in discussion of the restricted interest.
- Whenever the adolescent talked about an appropriate subject (relevant and not related to perseverations) for 30 seconds, the therapist would turn the card to green.
- The adolescent could then talk about whatever topic he wanted for 60 seconds.

- After that 60 seconds, the card was turned to red and the adolescent had to talk about something more appropriate during the therapy sessions.
- If he did not, then the therapist would ignore him briefly and the card would stay red until the adolescent talked about something appropriate for 30 seconds.
- This approach helped to decrease the amount of perseverative speech that the adolescent used for the session. It did not stop the adolescent perseverating entirely, but did decrease the amount and duration of perseverating during session.

Red Card, Green Card Exercise

Here are a set of steps for this Red/Green Card Exercise. You can use it during therapy or counseling sessions to specifically address perseverative and stereotyped behaviors. Bring it up to your client as an exercise you are using to help address problems that they are having with these specific types of behaviors.

1. Tell the client that you are going to do an exercise to work on perseverative behaviors.

2. Get one red card and one green card.

3. Hold up the Green card.

4. While the Green card is present, the client can talk about whatever subjects they want (including perseverative subjects).

5. After 30 seconds, hold up the Red card.

6. During that 30 seconds ignore the client when they perseverate.

7. When the client goes 30 seconds without an inappropriate subject, turn the card to Green.

8. After 60 seconds, hold up the Red card; keep it up until the client talks about something appropriate (and not related to perseveration) for 30 seconds.

9. For a client with stereotyped behaviors, this approach could be modified to reinforce the client avoiding stereotypic behaviors.

Behavioral Strategies

Designing effective strategies for addressing repetitive behaviors involves identifying which of the factors I identified previously might be contributing to the behaviors. You need to identify the reinforcers (e.g., decreased stress, physical stimulation) that are helping to keep the behaviors in place. You also need to identify whether there are any ways that the behaviors can be used to help increase other behaviors targeted in your therapy or counseling sessions.

Identifying what is keeping behaviors in place and what might be effective ways of addressing behaviors is at the very heart of applied behavior analysis. Ivy and Schreck (2016) found that applied behavior analysis, often studied as a treatment of choice for young children with autism, is an effective treatment throughout the life span.

This includes addressing perseverative and stereotypical behaviors in teenagers and adults with autism. In a meta-analysis of behavioral interventions for autistic symptoms, Roth, Gills and Reed (2014) found solid and consistent evidence of support for these interventions when used to treat perseveration and stereotyped behaviors.

Effective applied behavioral analysis typically starts with a comprehensive functional analysis. This is an important step for identifying what is keeping a problem behavior in place and is also essential for choosing essential treatment strategies (Boyd, McDonough & Bodfish, 2012).

There are multiple steps associated with a solid functional behavioral assessment. They involve identifying specific behaviors and the antecedents and consequences of those behaviors. The following worksheet is one that you can use to help conduct a solid functional behavioral assessment of perseverative and/or stereotyped behaviors that your clients exhibit.

Functional Behavioral Assessment

Identify the specific behavior being targeted (be as specific as possible):

_____

In at least five situations, identify what occurred prior to the behavior:

1. _____

2. _____

3. _____

4. _____

5. _____

In those five same situations, identify specifically what occurred after the behavior. (Note: Do not worry here about whether this seemed to reinforce the behavior, just note what occurred):

1. _____

2. _____

3. _____

4. _____

5. _____

Based on the data you collected, identify what seems to be the most consistent antecedent and consequence of the specific behavior:

A. _____

B. _____

C. _____

Response Interruption and Redirection

The Red Card, Green Card Exercise is a useful therapy technique for helping to reduce perseverative and stereotyped behaviors. It can be useful in therapy sessions, but you may also need additional interventions to help lessen repetitive behaviors that occur in school or in other settings. Response Interruption and Redirection (RIR) is an approach that has been found helpful for addressing repetitive behaviors in the setting in which they occur (Cassella, Sidener & Progar, 2011).

RIR focuses on interrupting the repetitive behavior quickly and abruptly, and then immediately getting the person to focus on another (predetermined) behavior. It is similar to the behavioral treatment for anxiety called "thought stopping" that involves helping the person with anxiety to yell "Stop" to themselves when they are ruminating on topics that make them anxious.

Determining the alternative behavior to use is done ahead of time. In RIR the person who addresses the repetitive behaviors is the one who tells the teenager or young adult what alternative behavior to use, but it should be a behavior that has been worked out with the teenager or young adult.

This way, he or she will know already (and be okay with) what is expected when the teacher intervenes to address the repetitive behaviors. Some alternative behaviors that I have heard to be effective include using some form of stress ball or plush toy that the person squeezes as an alternative means of getting some form of physical stimulation.

Here are the specific steps that are used with RIR:

- Observe repetitive behaviors (e.g., repeating statements from a favorite television show)
- Say the individual's name loudly (but not yelling) and clearly
- Gain eye contact with the individual
- Give instruction for the alternative behavior (e.g., "Squeeze the stress ball")
- Provide a positive statement to reinforce behavior (e.g., "Good job," "Yes!" or "That's right")

Differential Reinforcement of Alternative Behaviors

Other studies have looked at additional behavioral approaches for reducing perseverative and stereotyped behaviors. Of note are those with a behavioral plan that includes several different behavioral approaches that can be used to lessen the duration severity of the behavior problems.

Rehfeldt and Chambers (2003) published a case study of an adult with autism who was seen for behavior treatment. They observed that social attention tended to reinforce that individual's verbal perseverative behaviors. However, the techniques Differential Reinforcement of Alternative Behaviors (DRA) and extinction reduced the frequency of those behaviors.

DRA is a behavioral approach where the effective reinforcer (in this case, attention) is provided in response to the desired social behaviors (e.g., talking about the topic others are discussing) rather than the perseverative behaviors.

Extinction is the behavioral approach where attention is not provided when the targeted behaviors (e.g., the perseverative behaviors) occur. This is consistent with another case summarized in Wilder et al. (2001) showing that DRA and extinction can be used to decrease the frequency of inappropriate speech.

When using DRA for addressing perseverative and stereotyped behaviors, you focus on a behavioral plan in which your client is reinforced for using behaviors other than their problem behaviors for handling situations where the problem behaviors are likely to occur. If, for example, your client is in a social situation and is not talking about their preservative topic, then you would provide reinforcement for this behavior.

Here's another example: Let's say you are trying to increase the amount of time that your client can converse on subjects not related to their perseveration without needing to be prompted. Making use of DRA, you could set specific goals for the length of time they converse without perseverating. Then you can gradually increase that amount of time.

This is an intervention that can be made to work outside of the clinic. You will need to review the intervention with caregivers, focusing on how to extend the amount of time that the client successfully avoids perseverating before they receive the positive praise (or other reinforcement).

Notice that with the use of DRA, you still need to establish the pattern of when this problem behavior occurs and under what circumstances it occurs. Conducting a functional behavioral assessment is important for discovering: 1) when the reinforcement needs to be put in place, and 2) the circumstances in which your client is successfully using alternative behaviors rather than engaging in stereotyped or perseverative behaviors.

If social attention is a reinforcer for perseverative or stereotyped behaviors, then taking away that attention is a reasonable way to address it. This does not mean that ignoring the behavior will make it go away, but it does mean that lessening the attention given to the behaviors may make the duration shorter. If others are not giving attention to the behaviors, then it may mean that your client will not focus on the behavior and this could lessen the length of time that the behavior is reinforced.

Discussing extinction also brings up the (correct) notion that sometimes ignoring the perseverative or stereotyped behaviors is the best approach. If your client cannot do anything to stop the behavior, and if their caregivers cannot do anything to stop the behavior, then there really is no need to make the behavior stand out.

Giving the problem behavior less attention may lessen the reinforcement that helps it continue. But, even if that is not the case, people interacting with your client should remember that not making someone feel self-conscious for a behavior they cannot control is very often the right thing to do.

chapter 10

Working with Families, Spouses and Friends

I frequently find it difficult to work with the family members of teenagers and young adults. I realize that I have an obligation to help my clients with what they perceive to be problems. But sometimes their family members insist they know what my client really needs and want me to prioritize their concerns over my client's. It can be a challenging situation.

Parents or family members do not intentionally try to prevent their child from being able to make her or his decisions. But because their child has had difficulties their entire life, the parents have often had to answer for them; and that's a hard thing to give up. Autism presents considerable challenges and parents want to help their child navigate those challenges. In the past, this has meant having to speak for their child. Changing that can be difficult.

What makes it even more difficult is that teenagers and young adults with autism often look to their parents for direction—even if they are fully capable of making decisions on their own. They've spent so much of their lives assuming that their parents, or other family members, will answer questions for them that they don't even try to answer questions on their own.

When I ask my clients what they want to work on, they look to their parents for the answer. When they are encouraged to answer for themselves, they are often caught by surprise.

And at the beginning of therapy, who am I to tell them to change that? Sure, I'm the guy telling parents or other family members that I'm there to help their child. But why should they believe me? I brought up earlier that there is no reason a new client should believe I can actually do anything to help. That's equally true for family members.

What reason do they have for believing, other than my telling them, that I really have their child's best interests at heart? They know that they care about their child but they don't really know anything about me (at least not at the beginning). So, helping families change how they fend for their child with autism, who is now not really a child but is a teenager or young adult, often starts off as a difficult endeavor.

Here's an example: Robert is a teenager with autism who received services throughout childhood. He is now 17 years old and a high school senior. During the interview he says he is depressed because his parents keep telling him that he needs more friends. He says he is happy with his social interactions but feels very negative about himself because he does not interact with his peers as much as everyone else tells him that he should.

However, the parents' view is the polar opposite. In their interview, they say that Robert needs to have more friends. They realize that Robert says he is doing fine with his very small social circle, but they think that Robert does not really know what he needs. They emphasize that: He has needed help throughout his life, so how much does he know about what he really needs? We (his parents) have watched out for him throughout his life and we've seen what will make him happy. Besides, his sister is a college freshman and has a lot of friends and goes to a lot of parties. Robert needs to do that more.

Robert's example shows how difficult it can be to provide therapy in a session that involves both the client and their family members. Both your client and their family members may think they know what is best. And they both may look at you with suspicion if you don't take their side.

Working with a client's support system in therapy or counseling is often a balancing act between maximizing the help your client receives and respecting your client's desire for independence.

As in Robert's case, you may be working with a client who wants more independence but whose family doesn't think they are ready for it. It's important to ensure that family, friends and spouses are involved as needed, but also that they do not take over completely for your clients.

You will need to set expectations up front with family members regarding how much they should expect to be involved in decision making versus deferring decision making to your client. You also have to make sure that your client is being realistic about the amount of focus placed on what they want versus what the parents (or other family members) think is needed.

Family Members and Client Privacy

Prior to the first session with a teenager or young adult with autism, it is important to establish who will be attending the sessions. It may be that the parent who calls to make the appointment plans to come into sessions. For parents of teenage clients, this is to be expected. That would also be expected if the parent is the guardian of an adult who has been declared, legally, unable to make decisions.

If the client is considered to be an independent adult, you will need to make sure the parents know that the client will have to give approval for them to participate in sessions. Below is an example script for parents that can be helpful:

> *I can schedule the appointment with you. But you need to know that I will have to talk with (client's name) before we start to make sure he/she is OK with you being in the session. This is because he/she is considered legally an adult and has to give permission for others to join in the session. I don't expect this will take more than a minute, but I do need to explain this to him/her and get his/her permission before we start. I am legally required to do this.*

Although this script may seem straightforward, it can cause some difficulties depending on how prepared the family is to accept that their child is an adult (or close to being an adult).

They may have spent so much of their lives helping their child that the idea that their child is expected to make a decision—even if it is just about who comes into the therapy session—can be emotionally overwhelming. If you get a sense of surprise or frustration when addressing this issue with a family member, one useful approach is to explain that this legal requirement is a result of their child's age. A script can be helpful:

> *I can tell this caught you a little off guard. I just want to assure you this is not necessarily a major issue. It's just that your child is over 18 (or close to 18) and legally considered (or close to being legally considered) an adult. That just means that before the session begins, I will have to get his/her permission about who is allowed into the session—just as I would have to get your permission if this was your session. I doubt this will be a problem. It shouldn't take more than a minute for me to get the permission. If there is any problem I will address it then and there, and we will get it all straightened out.*

When they arrive for the first session, you can ask the client for permission to allow their parents to attend the session. If at all possible, you might want to see if your client will meet with you privately, even if only very briefly. If even that's too uncomfortable for them, then you can meet with everyone together and just ask:

> *I know you came here with your parents. I just want to make sure it's OK with you that we all meet together. This is a session to help you and you can have anyone in the session you want. Is it OK with you if I meet with you and your parents together?*

Even after you get your client's permission to get family members in the session, it is still important to set boundaries for parents and to provide them with an expectation of how much they should be involved. As we saw from the chapters on specific interventions, it is often helpful to have family members check to see that your client is practicing the skills that are presented in sessions.

So, as you work on new skills with your client, you want the parents to be aware of the specific skills your client is learning. But you also want to make sure that the focus is on the client learning the skills and not on the parents learning the skills. Keeping the parents involved, but not too involved, is an important balance to keep in session.

Here is a sample letter for parents that outlines their role both in and out of sessions. You might give this letter to the parents to look over while you are discussing permissions with the client.

Dear Family Member:

Thank you very much for coming in to help with your family member's treatment. It shows how much you care for them and how much they can depend on you to help.

I know that you want your family member to get all the help they can. During the sessions there will be times when I look for your input and depend on your help. But there will also be times when the focus is solely on your family member, and during that time your involvement will be more limited.

Here are some guidelines to help you understand the best ways to help your family member (the client) during sessions:

- *As I may have already explained to you, I need to get the client's full agreement to have you involved. This in no way questions your commitment to helping your family member. But because they are over 18 and considered to be an adult, I am legally required to have their consent.*

- *I often find that a family member's biggest role in this therapy is to help the client use the approaches we work on outside of session. You may very well need to remind the client of specific things we discussed during sessions and prompt them to use these approaches at home or out in the community. During session, it will be very important for me to talk as much as possible with your family member to help them understand what I am trying to get them to do. It will be equally important for you to pay attention to what I am trying to get your family member to do so that you can help them do the same thing at home.*

- *I will also depend on you to report what problems or progress you observed since the last session. I will be very interested to hear your perspective of what went on with your family member and what seemed to stand out as the most important happenings since the last session.*

- *Don't worry if what you recall is different from what your family member reports. It's not a cause for concern. Very often people have different views of the same events. Please refrain from making any negative comments if what your family member reports does not match what you recall. I assure you I will discuss this during session and try to reach a consensus on what needs to be addressed. But it is best to do this in a supportive way rather than jumping in and risk sounding critical.*

If you have any questions about any of these issues please do not hesitate to let me know.

_____   _____

Therapist's signature   date

_____

Therapist's name

Even if your client doesn't come in with family members, it may still be important for you to have contact with their parents or siblings. This is because parents may be very active in the client's life, even if they don't participate in sessions. As you obtain permissions from the client, you will also want to establish the amount of contact and type of contact you can have with family members.

From a clinician's point of view, it is useful for you to be able to share your recommendations with family members, to hear from them about the client's progress, and to check that they are doing what they can to help your client use approaches outside of sessions. Your client will need to approve each of these types of interactions.

It's a good idea to say specifically to your client that you are most likely to help them if you can have regular contact with family members outside of sessions. Being very direct about this can make clear to your clients that it's best for them to give permission for you to talk with family members if they do not have any definite and strong reason for you not to.

On the next page is a worksheet that you and the client can use to specify who you can talk to and what type of information you can share. It's not a legal form with the same legal standing as an authorization sheet. You will still need to have your client sign a formal authorization form giving permission for you to speak with specific family members. This is more of a therapeutic tool where you and your client specifically agree who you can involve to help make therapy more effective.

Notice that this sheet can be used to include family friends or even spouses. They can be added in the Other Family Members section, or it can be modified to specifically add those as choices.

Family Member Involvement

Client Name: _____

I give (therapist's or counselor's name) permission to discuss my treatment and recommendations with the following individuals:

_____ Mother Name:

_____ Father Name:

_____ Brother(s) Name(s):

_____ Sister(s) Name(s):

_____ Other Family Member(s) Name(s):

I give permission for (therapist's or counselor's name) to talk with these people about what I learn in sessions. This is so they can help me practice using these skills when I am home or doing something outside of my home.

Initial one of the following:

_____ I fully agree with the above statement

_____ I agree with the above statement except for the following:

Family Involvement

Even when adults with autism live alone there is often a great deal of continued and regular contact with immediate families (Krauss, Seltzer & Jacobson, 2005). This may change if the family member gets married but that doesn't happen very often. (Adults with autism do get married but at a much lower rate than adults without autism.)

A study of adults with autism in France (Chamak & Bonniau, 2016) found that all the individuals, ranging from severe to high-functioning autism, remained dependent on their parents throughout adulthood. As parents and children aged, the parents began to worry about the future of their children with autism.

They worried there would come a time when they could no longer provide support for their children who were still dependent and unable to look after themselves. This can end up putting stress on other family members who are asked to assume the supporting role.

As individuals with autism reach adulthood, families tend to move away from problem-focused services for the client, asking instead for emotion-focused help for themselves (Seltzer, Shattuck, Abbeduto & Greenberg, 2004). As a family member with autism gets older, parents and other family members often look for reassurance that things will work out. They may also ask for coping strategies for themselves to help them deal with concerns about their child.

As they shift away from problem-based services, parents will often focus more on their child's strengths than on their perceived weaknesses. As a therapist or counselor, you are in a good position to recognize any potential strengths that family members might have missed. By helping them to recognize and acknowledge their child's strengths and abilities, you give them reasons to be hopeful that these can be further strengthened as therapy continues. They will gain additional reassurance during your periodic updates when you provide your client's progress in both developing better skills and using those skills outside of sessions.

Other Family Members

It is useful to note that family members may attend your client's treatment session, in part, to get advice on difficulties that other family members may be having. There tends to be a higher rate of social deficits in siblings of individuals with autism compared to other groups of siblings (Seltzer, Krauss, Orsmond & Vestal. 2000). In addition, research by Mazefsky, Folstein and Lainhart (2008) found that relatives of individuals with autism have higher rates of affective disorders than both the general population and families of children with other developmental conditions. And so, family members may be struggling under the weight of multiple family issues and seek out your help.

It's worth your time to help them. Therapists and counselors can help to lessen the stress parents feel about their children with autism by addressing other issues that the family is experiencing. Sometimes family members put all their focus on the issues related to autism when there are equally problematic issues facing other family members.

Allowing parents the time to talk about all the issues facing members of the household (not just those related to your client with autism) and helping them work out a plan for addressing those issues can help ease the overall level of household stress. In the end, this can help lessen the degree of concern they have about your client and allow you more freedom to work on your client's issues without family interference.

Family Services

Parents may get over-involved in your client's treatment, often to the point of interfering, because they are concerned about other needs your client might have. Helping parents locate needed services for their child with autism can also help to decrease family stress.

Weiss, Tint, Paquette-Smith and Lunsky (2016) found that a large percentage of parents of adolescents and adults with autism experience difficulty accessing appropriate services for their children. This often contributes to these parents' emotional difficulties and feelings that they are not being successful in their attempts to help their children.

Given the crucial role that parents often play in the lives of individuals with autism spectrum disorders across the lifespan, it's important that service providers support the efforts of parents who provide and access care for their children.

Research has shown that, compared to parents of adults with other types of disabilities, parents of adults with autism experience a "worse" state of well-being. Parents often find themselves distressed because the time and effort they spend trying to get services for their children with autism interferes with their ability to plan for the future.

This in turn limits the parents' abilities to get their child involved in the community and to learn community-based skills that would allow them to be more independent.

In their study of parents taking care of an adult family member with autism, Burke and Heller (2011) found that increased future-planning and community involvement resulted in greater caregiving satisfaction.

Increasing community involvement for a family member with autism is often difficult for parents and siblings. Appropriate community activities, ones that provide sufficient structure and support to help make the activities beneficial, are often difficult to find. And this is not a difficulty that lessens even if the family member has intact intellectual functioning. Taylor and Seltzer (2011) found that young adults with autism without an intellectual disability were three times more likely to have no daytime activities compared to adults with autism who had an intellectual disability.

Work activities often increase community involvement and can offer a great deal of benefit for improving independent living skills. Getting a job can be beneficial for someone with autism but finding an appropriate job, again one that provides appropriate structure and support, is also often difficult. And involvement in work activities often decrease as individuals with autism get older.

Taylor and Mailick (2014) found significant declines in involvement with these types of activities as they studied a group of adults with autism over a period of 10 years. This underscores the need to try and address involvement in vocational and educational programs whenever possible during early adult years.

All of this shows how important it is for you as a counselor or therapist to help family members find and make use of community services. This can involve helping find appropriate community activities for your clients and/ or assisting in finding jobs or job training opportunities. It usually would be preferable to have a case manager involved in getting these services. But even if that's not possible, it's worth your time to help the family members find appropriate activities and services. Doing so can improve your client's community-based skills and help improve their lives.

Legal Adulthood

Legal adulthood is another issue relevant to the discussion of clients' independence. Once an individual reaches the age of 18 they are considered legally an adult and legally able to make their own decisions. An unusual exception is when a legal guardianship has been established, with typically the parents named as guardians. Your clients may not be aware of the legal implications, and you might find yourself being the first person to explain to parents that the child they have taken care of for the past 18 years is now legally considered able to make their own decisions. Families can find it hard to accept this.

It may also be difficult for your client with autism to accept that, after years of family members making decisions for them, they now have to step up and make decisions themselves. Clients can certainly acknowledge they want their parents involved and give their authority to parents to make decisions for them. But even in this case it will usually fall on you to ask your client whether they agree with what their parents said.

Explaining to parents up front that their adult child has to be involved with every decision made in sessions should be done with delicacy. Parents may need time to come to terms with the implications, as well as to express their frustrations about this. But if you make it clear that the legal entry into adulthood is based on age and not on the therapist's opinion, then they will have an easier time accepting the situation.

If you think that your client lacks the cognitive ability to make their own decisions, you should work with the parents to find help to establish the parents' legal right to continue as guardians. (In the U.S.A., this determination is usually made based on the individual's competence or decisional capacity.) You can help parents by assisting them in obtaining legal paperwork and obtaining a list of attorneys specializing in healthcare decision making.

Friend Involvement

All the issues addressed in this chapter also apply to close friends and spouses. Friends may, at times, want to know how to best help your client, and they may want to be involved in your client's treatments. This is fine provided that it is also something that your client wants. You will need to use the same process to get permission for friends to be involved that you used with family members.

Many times the friend who requests to be a part of a client's sessions is a family friend who has been involved with the client for much of their lives. This is often true for family friends who are called Aunt or Uncle but are not biologically related to your client.

In these cases it is even more important to make sure that your client recognizes what having these individuals in the therapy sessions might mean. Having close family friends involved in making sure that approaches are used effectively outside of sessions is helpful provided that your client reciprocates the friendship. Taking some extra time talking with your client alone to make sure that they see these relationships as supportive, positive and trusting helps eliminate potential future difficulties.

When the friends wanting to be a part of the session are your client's peers then it may very well be that they are hoping to understand their friend better. Giving the friend a general explanation of what autism is can be helpful. But make sure to talk about autism as more of a different way of interacting with people rather than necessarily being a problem. You don't want to make your client's behaviors stand out in more of a negative way to your client's friends than might already be the case.

After first giving them a general explanation of autism, allow them to ask specific questions. By doing this, you are focusing the session on what the peer wants to know about their friend and their individual situation rather than on what you assume that the peer needs to know to be helpful. Taking the time to do this will also help your client.

Spousal Involvement

Spouses present unique situations in sessions for adults with autism. Adults with autism do not get married frequently but when they do their lack of comprehension of social interactions often causes issues to arise. These are challenges that need to be worked out because, unlike with parents or friends, the goal is **not** to get your client to lessen a reliance on this other person.

Spouses should be strongly encouraged to attend sessions. This does not mean that every session has to be a marital session, but therapy sessions should address issues in the marriage whenever possible. It's a very good idea for the couple to receive marital therapy even if it coincides with you still working individually with your client. This allows you to address the difficulties facing the client individually, while being comfortable that the marital relationship is also being addressed.

chapter 11

Generalization

We've all seen it. A client comes in to session, motivated for change. You work with them and they make great progress—*in session*. They can identify how they are going to deal with problems and how they are going to keep new problems from occurring. They can verbalize a clear plan—*in session*.

But then your client goes out into the real world and everything comes crashing down. All their plans go to pot and nothing you talked about in session comes into play. Your client had all these great plans that they could verbalize *in session,* but then when reality hits them they can't make it happen.

Perhaps you have a client who has problems getting along with someone at work. They get into loud arguments with this person and it really disrupts their workday. Your client is on the verge of getting fired and they really need to turn things around. You work with them on specific strategies to deal with this co-worker and (*Hooray!!*) they work. Your client finds effective ways of avoiding the arguments and the problems at work go away.

But then your client has problems with a neighbor. This neighbor keeps parking in his or her spot. Your client ignores it, very briefly, but then just decides they can't take it anymore. So they get into arguments with the neighbor. Really loud arguments. These arguments occur at all hours, wake up other neighbors, and the police are called.

What happened? In each case your client knew what to do in one situation. Why didn't this carry over to another? Why could they say what they needed to do at one time but then not actually do it at another? Where did all that understanding and knowledge go?

All of this relates to the process called generalization. This is the process where an individual takes something that they learned in one setting and applies it in another setting. In many ways, it is the very essence of what you are trying to do in therapy and counseling. You are trying to help the person learn new skills in session that they can use for dealing with situations they face outside of session.

Generalization is essential for therapy and counseling, but you can see its importance if you consider other professions as well. Imagine you are a high school history teacher and the class is studying the civil war. If you can get students to learn who won the war, that is great. But if they only remember the information in the classroom then it's essentially worthless.

What is important is not just that students learn the information, but that they can use it in many other places (for example, relating a fact from history to a similar current event). The same goes for therapy and counseling.

Generalization & Autism

Autism significantly impacts a person's ability to generalize. There are a number of theories about why this is true and most of them relate to neurological factors associated with autism. Discussing these neurological factors is beyond the scope of the book and that is in part because there is a lot of disagreement about which specific aspects of autism's neurology impact generalization. It would take almost an entire book to discuss all these theories. But there is a lot of research to support the notion that generalization is a major problem with autism.

One example of this research is a study by Froelich et al. (2013). They compared young adults with high-functioning autism to typically-developed peers. They found that the adults with autism showed significant difficulty applying what they learned in one situation to a new situation. This problem increased as the situations became increasingly less similar to the original situation.

A review of the literature by deMerchena, Eigsti and Terys (2015) found that verbally fluent teenagers with autism had significantly more difficulty than matched peers in learning from their experiences and applying these new skills to other types of situations.

Teenagers and young adults with autism especially have difficulty with generalization. There are several possible reasons for this:

- Individuals in their teenage and young adult years can often be resistant to using new approaches. They may become comfortable with the approaches they have used to manage problems and may be hesitant to try new approaches, in part because they fear failure or fear they will call attention to their problems, or they may just not want to.

- As we've addressed many times in this book, many of the problems individuals with autism face in their teenage and younger adult years are much more complex than those they experienced in childhood. This increased complexity can make it more challenging to figure out how exactly to apply the interventions in one setting to other types of situations.

- Motivation for improving behaviors can be more limited for teenagers and young adults if they do not see an immediate need. For example, teenagers with autism may "hear" adults tell them they need to improve their social skills but, unless they have identified specific problems, the teenagers may not really see a strong need to put much effort into changing.

As a way of illustration, here's an example of a therapy case where generalization is a concern:

Case Study
Generalization

Robert, an 18-year-old senior in high school, has been in therapy with a psychologist for three months. He began therapy primarily because of yelling episodes with other students at his high school. Robert's parents and the staff at his school were concerned that if he didn't develop better skills for dealing with anger in social situations he wouldn't be able to function in other school or work environments.

Robert has actively participated in therapy sessions and has responded positively to the anger management interventions his therapist has used to help him. But lately his parents and therapist have expressed concern because he hasn't actually used any of these skills for dealing with anger at school. When talking about situations in therapy sessions, he has done well at identifying approaches he could use for handling anger. However, he has not shown evidence of consistently using those approaches when confronted with a difficult situation. He has not yet learned to generalize what he knows to new situations.

Five Aspects of Therapy to Maximize Generalizations

In the remainder of this chapter, I'm going to look at ways to help address generalization issues (like those presented by Robert) in therapy and counseling. These approaches are geared to maximize the likelihood that the lessons your clients with autism learn in session are actually used outside of session and in different types of problem situations.

Neely et al. (2016) conducted a review of the research on generalization in autism and found five aspects of therapy and counseling approaches that are important for maximizing generalization:

1. Emphasize generalization at the start of the interventions
2. Focus interventions on teaching skills in the setting in which the problems would typically occur
3. Teach the skills across the different situations and the different stimuli that could possibly trigger problem behaviors
4. Allow the individual multiple opportunities to practice the skills
5. Collect data to test whether or not generalization is occurring

Let's take a look at each of these aspects, and see how they can be addressed in therapy and counseling sessions.

Addressing Generalization at the Start

Taking steps to maximize generalization starts at the beginning of therapy or counseling. When clients first enter therapy or counseling you want to get specific information about situations causing them difficulties. This gives you a starting place for understanding the types of situations that need to be addressed.

Here is an example of a question that I ask the individual or their parents to help identify situations that cause difficulties:

When you first called to set up this appointment what were two (or more) situations that occurred right before you decided to make this call? Even if you had been dealing with these problems for some time there clearly was something about these situations that made you decide that now you needed to move forward with setting up these sessions. I would like you to describe for me, in as much detail as you can, what happened in those situations.

On the next page is a worksheet that you can use to gather specific information about those situations. You want the person providing the information to be as specific as possible. You also want to leave your questions as open-ended as possible so that they can describe their particular experiences.

Description of Problem Situations

Talk with your client about different scenarios, and gather information. Encourage your client to be as specific as possible.

1. Describe the setting (e.g., school, home, activity, etc.) where problem behavior(s) occur. Please use as much detail as possible:

2. Describe the time of day or time of week when problems are most likely to occur:

3. Describe who is typically involved in the situation:

4. Describe any other important factors associated with the problem situation:

5. Describe the behaviors you have that cause you difficulties in this specific type of situation (e.g., hitting, yelling, walking away, crying, loud refusals, etc.):

It is best practice, in my opinion, to gather details of four situations that will provide a solid foundation for addressing most, if not all, of the general scenarios causing the person difficulties. You want to get as much real-world data as possible to help the person recognize the sorts of approaches they should take for dealing with problem situations.

One other thing about this worksheet is that it is similar to the establishing goals worksheet I provided in Chapter 3. It is meant to be an extension of that worksheet by providing more details about specifically where the person experiences problems. That earlier worksheet was meant to talk about goals while this one focuses on specifics so that you can decide early on what types of situations need to be targeted.

Teaching Across Different Situations

Now here comes the tricky part. And I call it tricky because, in my experience, it's the part where clients (or their families) are most likely to drop out of therapy or counseling.

You've identified the specific problems that led your client to come into sessions (or the family to bring your client in). And you've obtained specifics about the situations. But you know that the problems probably don't end there. You know that Robert's problems (from the case study) are probably due to anger management and not just to getting along with a few peers at high school.

You know this, but your client (or your client's family) doesn't necessarily know this (or want to admit it). Robert may know, "Yes, I've got problems with anger," or may say, "No, my problems are just with these jerks at high school." If you move too quickly into making the problem more than Robert is willing to make it then it's pretty likely Robert is going to say, "This person can't help me, they don't even know what my problem is."

All of this is important because this is where generalization comes in. Because, in order to help your client generalize, you need to help him or her see that their problems occur across different settings. Emphasizing generalization is important, but can be difficult if your client (or the family) does not see solutions as needing to be generalized.

So, the approach that you take in terms of addressing generalization will depend on your client's view of their problems. If your client views the problems as only occurring in certain situations, then you need to focus on just those situations first. To be honest, that is not my preferred approach. I prefer to start right off with talking about problems in the most general way possible so clients are prepared to look at generalizing skills right from the start. But if your client is not willing to do that, then what are you going to do?

If your client sees their problem only related to certain situations, then you need to wait until after you help them make some success before discussing generalization. You can instead work on exercises to help them deal better with the specific situations they bring up (like the arguing at school brought up in Robert's example). Once they see some success with anger management skills, then you can start to ask them about other situations causing problems.

What you are trying to do here is get your client to look at the different types of situations causing problems. You are trying to get him or her to see the big picture of their problems. Your client may not be willing to see this at the beginning, but you know she or he needs to get there.

If you are going to have your client investigate how to use new skills in situations where problems typically occur (from the steps listed earlier), then there needs to be a discussion of all the potential problem settings. You'll just have to decide if your client is ready to discuss this at the beginning of session or whether they need some success in handling the problems that brought them in before discussing problems more generally.

If you are unsure about how your client views this issue you are better off focusing on the problems that brought them in (and wait until later to discuss more general problems). This keeps the focus on what your client says the problem is, and eliminates the potential problem of them quitting therapy before they've seen some success.

Once you establish that your client is ready to talk about problems on a more general scale, the following worksheet can be helpful. It is designed to help discuss problems other than the initial ones they brought into therapy. You can use the worksheet to look at situations that are similar to the ones your client ran into and that suggest the general difficulties they face.

Potentially Problematic Situations

You can use this worksheet to look at situations similar to the ones they listed on the Description of Problem Situations. Notice how the descriptions focus on situations that occurred or they think might occur given the problems they've identified.

For this worksheet, describe in as much detail as you can what has happened in this situation OR (if you have not actually faced the situation recently) what you think would happen in this situation.

Describe the setting in as much detail as possible:

_____

_____

Describe when it is most likely to occur:

_____

_____

Describe who is most likely to be involved in that situation:

_____

_____

Describe how other people are acting in that situation:

_____

_____

Describe other factors that you think are important to consider:

_____

_____

Practicing Skills

When it's time to move from identifying problem situations to learning and using effective skills, the two most effective therapy approaches are role-playing exercises and self-monitoring exercises.

Role-playing is the most effective way to help your client practice skills before actually putting them into place outside of session. You will be doing role-playing in two steps. You will want to discuss situations that the person is likely to run into, and the scenarios identified in the first worksheet are a good place to start. You will use these scenarios to work with the client to identify approaches that can be used to avoid difficulties in the future.

There are two things to keep in mind about role-playing exercises. First, you want your client to reach the point where they can identify, on their own, how to use approaches. That's the goal of step one.

Even if you have to work with them a number of times, it is important that they can identify on their own how they can use these approaches. But, it is also important to keep in mind that this is usually where the process of generalization breaks down. Remember the case example with Bob that was described earlier in which he was unable to see the generalization, he lost faith in his therapist and he stopped making progress.

Once the individual is able to independently identify approaches to use in the scenarios in the first worksheet, you can move to the second worksheet and the second step. The second worksheet has variations of the scenarios that were used in the first step. The client's goal in step two is to independently identify approaches for effectively handling these variant situations.

Scenarios on the second worksheet should be similar to those in the first but also contain enough differences that they can aid the process of generalization. The idea is to prompt the individual to recognize the types of situations that are likely to cause them difficulty and to recognize the variations in these new situations.

This is one of the reasons that it is useful to have multiple examples of potentially problematic situations. You can use different examples for each of the two steps. That is, you can use some of the examples for prompting the client on how to use the approaches, and then use the remaining examples for sessions in which they try to identify how to deal effectively with situations on their own.

Once you have reached the point where your client is able to discuss how he or she would handle a potentially problematic situation on their own (with only minimal prompting from you) then you are ready to move on to the next step: self-monitoring.

In a study of four adolescents who were learning vocational social skills, Kelly et al. (1983) found that although role-playing helped with learning skills, it was self-monitoring that helped with skills generalization. They found that training without making use of self-monitoring produced very poor generalizing skills outside the training sessions. However, when they asked the adolescents 1) how often they used the skills they just learned and 2) how effective those skills were for dealing with problem situations, the training results improved.

Self-monitoring is used right in the session. And you can incorporate it into sessions even before teaching the client self-prompting. This is because just the process of keeping track of how often you are doing something that is effective increases the number of times you use those skills to address real-life problems.

The therapy process often occurs once the person actively pays attention to how often they make use of the skills taught in session. You can help move this process along by having the individual start using the self-monitoring worksheet on page 167 as soon as possible after skills are taught.

Let's take eye contact as an example. One of the steps you might take with a client who is having social problems would be initiating and maintaining eye contact when speaking with someone. Even if this is a problem for your client, it is not necessarily going to be the case that he or she recognizes up front that this is an issue (he or she might notice that people do not respond positively when he or she talks to them but may not know why).

You can help by pointing out to your client what you notice about his or her lack of eye contact. You could also share how it makes you feel (and how you might want to respond) when she or he does not keep eye contact when talking with you.

This leads to self-monitoring exercises where you can help your client pay attention to eye contact and keeping that eye contact throughout conversations during session. Addressing that your client is monitoring his or her use of appropriate and effective social behaviors, like maintaining eye contact, is helpful to do not just during session but also during small talk after session or discussions about setting up the next appointment.

You are keeping focused during each interaction on helping your client pay attention that she or he is actually using social behaviors you discussed. You helped your client with a social behavior even before he or she leaves the office and set up a good self-monitoring exercise to continue after your client leaves the office.

Multiple Opportunities

Once you get through identifying problem situations, both those that the client has actually faced and those you feel they might face, then you can move on to skills training for handling those situations. During training, you could use any, or all, of the approaches described in this book. What's important is that the client develop some understanding of how she or he can handle the problem situations they identified.

No matter what approaches you take, after practicing skills in session, it's time to get the person to use the skills. A key ingredient to achieving success is the use of prompting the person to use skills outside of session. There are a number of ways to implement prompting.

A teacher, mentor or family member can occasionally remind the person to use their new skills. Likewise, a therapist or family member can text the client randomly throughout the day. Or the client can prompt themselves using prerecorded prompts (either audio or visual). The eventual goal is for the client to independently remind themselves (without the use of any other individual or equipment) to use the skills outside of session.

There are basically two types of prompts used in therapy or counseling with individuals who have autism:

1. Randomly prompt the person to use skills (e.g., social skills to initiate and maintain conversations) at different times throughout each day.

2. Randomly prompt the person to check on how they are feeling (e.g., how angry are they at the moment) and then have them decide (based on how they are feeling) whether they need to take steps for addressing problems covered in sessions. This usually occurs with your client using

a pre-chosen rule for when certain steps will be put into place. An example might be that the person uses specific steps of a mindfulness exercise if he or she decides his or her anger is at 6 or above on a anger scale of 1–10.

Prompts will usually involve you, as the person's therapist or counselor, prompting her or him in session and then a family member or spouse prompting them to use skills outside of the sessions. But many times you will be working with someone who doesn't have anyone to help with the prompting.

In that case, you can set up a schedule where you prompt the person to use skills at different times of the day. Some ideas include: Have your client record himself or herself on their smartphones or computer tablets along with a prompt of what it is that they should be doing. Or you could have the person use handwritten index cards containing the steps they can take to more effectively deal with problem situations.

On the following page are some examples of different types of prompts a person might use for handling situations outside of therapy.

Different Types of Prompts

Therapist Prompt (in-session):

Now that we reviewed the situation you had problems with before, I want you to think about how you would use the steps we discussed so far for handling that situation.

Therapist Prompt (outside of session):
(Note: This would involve the therapist or counselor sending a text message at different times during the week prompting the individual to use specific skills.)
Go up to the next person you recognize, greet them and ask them how their day is going. Be sure to make it clear that you are interested in what they are saying.

OR

Write down your rating of how angry you are right now. If it is more than 3 (using the scale we talked about in session) then use the anger management skills we discussed.

Family Member Prompt:
This looks like the type of situation that you talked about in therapy when you talked about anger. Even if you do not feel angry right now, go through the steps that you learned in therapy for this type of situation.

Self-Prompt:
(Note: This would involve use of visual or text reminders.)
Remember to count backwards from 10 when you feel like you want to hit something.

Collecting Data

After skills training and working out a plan for prompting, it's time to shift your focus to collecting data. You need to know how consistently your client is using the skills outside of session. Oftentimes, the therapist will provide the client with a notebook where he or she (or his or her family member) can note when they used the skills, why (in what situations) they used the skills, what specific skills they used, and how severe of a problem they faced.

For the severity, you could use a scale from 0–10, with 0 meaning no problems and 10 meaning the most problems they could imagine. You want the individual to provide the data about severity both before and after using the skills. This data will give you feedback on when your client is using skills covered in sessions and allow you to address what steps your client can take to increase the effective use of those skills.

Following is a worksheet that your client can use to collect the necessary data.

Data Collection Sheet

Situation	Day & Time	Severity (0–10)	Skills Used	Severity

Initiation

Once clients have shown the ability to use effective skills with prompting from others, then they are ready to enter into the "initiation" phase of therapy or counseling. This is where your clients keep track of taking steps on their own without prompting from others. It is the final step of generalization and the step in which your client is actually using the new skills on their own.

Rosenberg, Congdon, Schwarts and Kamps (2015) provided a set of steps for initiating the use of social skills outside of social skills group training programs. They worked in a school setting and focused on having the students with autism use social skills during the recess breaks following lunch. Their method, called the Say-Do intervention, was found to help improve social skills. Here are the steps:

1. Identify (during the school day prior to lunch break) who the student will talk to during the break. This needs to be as specific as possible.
2. Keep track of who they talk to during the lunch break.
3. Have the individual use the specific skills they had learned in social skills group. (How these skills are to be used was discussed in Chapter 6.)
4. Review reinforcement for talking to the persons as planned.

Using Technology

Teenagers and young adults tend to enjoy new technology and this is no less the case with individuals who have autism. There are many different ways that technology can be used in therapy and counseling to help generalize skills that are addressed in sessions. This can include:

- Text messages to remind the individual to use specific skills at certain times of the day
- Audio reminders and prompts to use specific sets of skills to address situations faced at certain times
- Video instructions to help remind the individual how to use specific skills
- Scheduling and note taking programs to keep track of the effectiveness of different skills for dealing with potentially problematic situations

Using technology has been shown to help with generalization of different skills for teenagers and young adults with autism. For example, Alexander found that the use of video modeling helped individuals with autism learn how to sort mail. These individuals were shown videos on their mobile devices that walked them through the specific steps for sorting mail and also provided audio instructions. Their results showed that this use of video modeling helped with the generalization of skills from training to the work environment.

Other areas that have been shown to be positively impacted (in terms of improving generalizations) through the use of video instructions include:

- Social skills (Dauphin, Kinney, Stromer & Koegel, 2004)
- Communication skills (Wert & Neiswarth, 2003)
- Job skills (Mechling & Ortega-Hurndon, 2007)
- Daily-living skills (Lasater & Brady, 1995)

chapter 12

Preparing for Independent Living

Now we finally come to the point in which the client moves from learning skills for independence to actually taking steps to act more independently. Acting with greater independence means that the client:

1. Actively uses skills that are effective for interacting with other people

2. Communicates their wants and needs in a way that gets those wants and needs met

3. Reduces behaviors that prevent them from living life fully

For the client, living more independently means actually taking steps to live on their own—or, more accurately, to live on their own as much as they are able to.

This whole area gets into work that may not always seem to be work meant for therapists or counselors. Case managers, social workers and service coordinators are professionals that typically specialize in getting people the services they need to live independently, and these may be the professionals you refer clients to in order to get the services they need.

But your clients, and/or their families, may often look to you in order to help them interact effectively with the people who are trying to get them resources, or they may look to you for help in getting the services. There are several reasons why they may need your help.

Your clients may get so anxious and/or overwhelmed by following instructions from other people that you need to help them deal with this distress. Or it might be that your clients and their families disagree in some way about the road to independence and you may need to intervene. It also may be that there is just nobody available to help your clients and their families get what they need. You may not really see it as your job, but if there is no one else around to do it, what else are you going to do?

To be honest, I find case management work like this often frustrating and annoying. Not that I don't want to help my clients. But finding the necessary resources can be difficult. There are often different rules for different agencies and it is often not apparent what those rules are. There's also very little consistency about the types, function and availability of agencies in any given region. The search can be taxing, and stretch you far outside of your normal job responsibilities. You may not want to do it. But, again, if no one else is there to do it, what else are you going to do?

In this chapter, I will provide terms and information that can be useful during the search for services. Armed with this information, you and your client may find services and organizations that are well-suited to provide help for your client as he or she travels the road to independence.

Finding services to help with independent living (however that is defined) is usually done by case managers and service coordinators. These are specific titles for professionals who help clients locate services and walk them through the steps for obtaining services. Case manager is the most common title and service coordinator is often the title used for specific types of case managers. But some states use different titles and it can be confusing. If you are having difficulties finding a case manager, or determining if your state has different terms for case management professionals, you can contact your state's chapter of the Case Management Society of America (listed at www.cmsa.org).

Most states have organizations that are called Centers for Independent Living. These are organizations—usually nonprofits—that provide information about services that help individuals with disabilities live independently. Each state has different ways of providing information about these organizations but there are two government websites that may help you locate them: www.disability.gov and www.ssa.gov/work/WIPA.html.

Making Decisions About Independence

Before you start working with your client to achieve greater independence, you need to determine the types of independence he or she is ready for, and age is one factor to keep in mind. Daily-living skills for those with autism tend to improve during adolescence and early adulthood but then level out in their late 20s. Individuals with intellectual disabilities have a slower progression, and they may not show improvement or gain new skills until their early 20s (Smith, Maenner & Seltzer, 2012).

Anxiety and/or mood disorders may impede your client's ability to work towards independence. Matson et al. (2009) found that those with the combination of autism and intellectual disabilities have greater problems with adaptive skills than those with intellectual disabilities alone. But those who also have mood and/or anxiety disorders have greater problems yet. Fortunately, mood and/or anxiety disorders are often treatable, and if treatment is successful, you should see improvement in the effectiveness of your interventions for greater independence.

When trying to determine the level of independence your client might achieve, make use of the materials you gathered during your initial assessment. IQ scores, in particular, are a good reflection of ability since they typically do not change over time. Clients whose IQ scores fall in the intellectual disability range will most likely need more assistance throughout their lives, whereas clients whose IQ scores are more in the average range (even if it is the low average range) are more likely to be fully independent.

Use this information as a guide, and combine it with information gathered throughout your sessions, to determine the independence levels (e.g., employment, driving, cooking) your clients are likely to reach. And keep in mind that everyone is capable of some increased level of independence, even if full independence is not a realistic goal.

You also want to consider what more independence means to your client. One client may want to someday live on their own. Another client may want to work, but not necessarily live on their own. In the past, determining a person's independence potential took a one size fits all approach with a focus on specific outcomes related to friendships, employment and living arrangements. But, in recent years, research has shown the benefit of customizing the approach to measuring a person's potential (Henninger & Taylor, 2013).

Determining potential based on what's needed for an individual to fit into their immediate environment, as opposed to using an approach that assumes every person with autism's environment is similar, is currently showing more promise. Taking into account an individual's desire, and potential, for independence is a way of taking a more individualized approach towards independence.

The Independence Checklist will help you determine the types of independence that are within reach of your client. The worksheet itemizes the different levels of independence, such as employment, housing, cooking and driving, and lists the types of skills needed to achieve independence in each. The worksheet has room for your comments, including why you think they can gain that type of independence.

The worksheet becomes a useful document for discussing independence with your client and their family, and you may want to share your assessment and comments with them. That said, your clients and their family members may disagree with your viewpoint. Family members may need to be convinced that your client can do the things necessary to gain more independence.

For example, your client might show the capability and interest in finding a job. But family members, who may be used to seeing your client requiring help for mundane tasks, may not be so sure that they are ready for a job. You can use the notation section on the checklist to list the reasons why you think your client is capable of achieving a certain type of independence, and then share this with parents if they question your assessment.

A view that I have stressed throughout this book is that all of your clients, regardless of their abilities, want to reach their maximum level of independence. This is just the nature of being a teenager or young adult.

Even if you run through the Independence Checklist and do not mark any items, you will still want to work with clients and families to determine what tasks your clients are likely to be able to do on their own. That is the reason for the Other Areas section at the very end of the checklist. Use that section to address any very basic areas of independence that should be considered, especially if the main ones listed on the checklist are not appropriate. Some very basic examples include:

- Go shopping on their own every week
- Clean up the house
- Make phone calls for appointments
- Call to check on elderly neighbors
- Run errands in the neighborhood
- Volunteer at local community activities
- Take messages off the answering machine
- Walk the dog every day

Independence Checklist

Client Name: _____

Listed below are major areas of independence. There are also some examples of abilities associated with these areas. Write comments if you think the abilities are within reach for your client or if they need some improvement.

Examples	Sample Abilities	Comments
Employment	Show up on time, follow instructions, complete tasks in a timely manner, speak up when facing difficulties	
Live independently	Make appropriate decisions from multiple choices, call for help when needed from appropriate authorities, cook, clean, pick out clothes appropriately, monitor temperature in house and respond accordingly, make appropriate decisions regarding safety, handle free time without difficulties	
Live in group home	Follow instructions, cook, clean, get along appropriately with other people (not necessarily interact frequently, but get along), follow safety rules appropriately	
Drive a car	Appropriate level of manual dexterity, follow rules of the road, engage in tasks without being distracted, show appropriate car handling skills	

Examples	Sample Abilities	Comments
Use public transportation	Follow bus or subway schedule, plan for getting to stops in time, recognize appropriate stops for getting off bus or subway, ask for help if needed, keep from causing disruptions	
Cooking	Plan a menu, shop for ingredients, use a stove safely, follow cooking instructions, check food for temperature and doneness	
College or technical training	Learn material appropriately, take tests, adequately follow the classroom lessons, keep from causing distractions, living in a dorm room	
Other areas of independence worth considering		

Programs Supporting Independence

Let's look at examples of situations involving clients who want increased levels of independence. Your work with teenagers and young adults with autism might involve some, or all, of the following:

- A young adult with moderate intellectual disability and autism will probably live with his family all of his life, but still wants to do more things on his own. After you discuss this issue with your client and his family, you determine that he might thrive in a day program or a structured workshop. He may also need to be evaluated for a Social Security Disability to determine if obtaining financial assistance through disability payments is a possibility. Having both autism and intellectual disability does not guarantee qualification for disability payments but it is often worth looking into.

- A teenager with autism and mild intellectual disability in her junior year of high school knows that she will not be able to live on her own anytime soon, but wants to prepare for a job. She and her family have identified some local grocery stores that have clerking jobs she can handle, but she needs job training to learn effective work skills. She would also benefit from having a job coach to help her improve her job performance at whatever job she gets.

- A high school graduate with autism and an average IQ has been working at a local restaurant as a dishwasher, and is starting to train there as a line cook. He thinks this is a job he can enjoy and at which he can do well because it involves cooking but is also very structured. His goal is to not only do well at this job but also to live on his own. He wants to live near his parents but wants to be independent. He does not have concerns about his work skills, but he does not know how to go about finding his own apartment or how to obtain reliable transportation.

It's not hard to see the variety of issues you will face as you search for resources to help each of these individuals. Each client has different needs, and a resource capable of addressing one area may not be able to help you find ways of addressing other needs. In fact, it may be difficult to find resources to meet some of those needs.

Since there are different resources serving different regions, it is useful to have the names of national organizations with local offices. One organization that I find has a lot of useful material in a wide variety of areas is Autism Speaks. They are particularly helpful because they focus on resources throughout the life span. Their information is as focused on teenagers and adults (even older adults) as it is on children and younger teenagers.

You can look up a number of different types of resources and get information about those resources in different areas throughout the country.

Other national organizations that provide information about the types of services available nationally, but which also have local offices in many different areas, include:

- Autism Society (www.autism-society.org)
- National Autism Center (www.nationalautismcenter.org)
- National Autism Association (www.nationalautismassociation.org)
- Autism Now (The Arc) (www.autismnow.org)

School Services

Getting information from organizations working with individuals with autism is important. But, before you look into what those services have to offer, you will want to make sure your client is not eligible for services available in his or her school district. Keep in mind that throughout the country school districts are required to provide at least some services to students with special needs until about the age of 21.

This is important because even with help from the organizations I listed earlier, it can be hard to find support services for someone out of school. Many services are less available after graduation, and for those that are available, the waiting list can be long.

Schools are legally required to help students still eligible for their services and, because of this, the services typically have greater availability. So you'll want to make sure that your client looks into the services available in their school district before you move on to outside organizations.

Here are some examples of the services that schools might have available to help students become more independent:

- Classes on using public transportation
- Driving education services for students with special needs

- Vocational training for students with special needs
- Living skills training for individuals with special needs
- Financial classes regarding money-management skills (e.g., budgeting, using banking services) for students with autism

Make an effort to encourage clients and family members to ask school administration whether any of the services are available. Again, this is important given that these services are more readily available while the individual is a student in school, than after they graduate.

There are a few professional titles to keep in mind when it comes to getting services through a school. One is educational advocate. This is a professional with a specialized knowledge of educational law and what services schools are supposed to provide.

Having the help of an educational advocate can be very important if individuals or families have difficulty getting the services they are entitled to. I have found this type of professional particularly important when schools do not meet the requirements for providing services for students with special needs up until age 21.

Another common staff role in a school district is the transitions coordinator. This person's job is to help students figure out what steps they need to take to transition successfully from high school to secondary education, training programs, military or work. They work with all students, not just those with special needs, but they can be very helpful for students with special needs who are trying to figure out what to do after high school.

Transition coordinators often work closely with the government organization, Office of Vocational Rehabilitation (OVR), which helps individuals determine what skills and training they currently have that are useful in the workplace, and what additional training they need to best fit their potential in the market.

Finding Employment

Gaining employment represents a milestone for an individual with autism hoping to increase independence. Having a job provides an opportunity to not only feel independent, but also provides real opportunity to exert one's independence. This is why helping your clients with autism discover the types of employment that fit them is so important.

While many people with autism find jobs, it is still the case that the vast majority are unemployed or underemployed. This was shown to be true during a large study of employment in autism several years ago (Gerhardt & Lainer, 2011) and the situation has improved only a little since then.

There are a number of reasons why teenagers and young adults with autism are underemployed. School programs are oftentimes not set up to help the student with the practicalities associated with transitioning from adolescence to adulthood (Hendricks & Wehman, 2009). Work environments require social skills that often may not be specifically addressed in school programs.

Developing and maintaining positive social interactions may be stressed in school, but things like showing up on time and putting in a full day of work and effort may not be stressed. Maintaining focus on tasks for hours at a time without being distracted, or focusing instead on preferred activities, may also create difficulties.

Other reasons for underemployment in adults with autism are related to employers. There may be training programs available for individuals with autism to function in a work environment, but programs are less available to help employers recognize how best to work with their employees with autism. Having an employee with autism may present unique challenges that an employer is not ready to handle. It is not that addressing these challenges is overly complex but, in order to do so, the employer must be ready to help and know where to get important information.

There is a program out of England that provides services to help individuals with autism find jobs and also provide employers with guidance on inclusive practices and management approaches specifically for helping individuals with autism. The program is called the National Autistic Society (NAS) Prospects program. One study found this program helped 68% of its participants find employment over an eight-year period (Howlin, Alcock & Burkin, 2005), and included finding work for individuals with both higher and lower abilities.

Postsecondary Education

Many colleges offer programs to help students with autism be successful at school. One specific example is the College Program for Students with Autism

Spectrum Disorder at Marshall University in West Virginia. The program is specifically designed to help students work out social difficulties and to become successful at academic tasks that are often problematic for people with autism (e.g., asking professors for help, speaking up in class).

Although the majority of public and private universities these days offer support for students with autism, Marshall University is one example of a school whose program is more comprehensive. Examples of other colleges with similar types of comprehensive programs include:

- University of Alabama
- Texas Tech University
- Nova Southeastern University (Florida)
- Western Kentucky University
- Eastern Illinois University

For some of your clients, one step on the road to independence includes college, and you can help them prepare for it. College offers young adults with autism the opportunity to be more independent while either living at home or in a dormitory setting.

You can provide help to your client by encouraging them to contact the Student Affairs office at their school of choice to find out the name of the department that supports students with autism. They will want to take the lead in contacting the school and also in finding out what services are provided. You might suggest that they look at programs from several colleges so that they understand the types of support that their school of choice does, and does not, offer. Once they track down programs and services, they should ask for student and family handouts so that they have the information readily available.

It's important to understand that a program that provides services for those with special needs will not necessarily provide adequate services for students with autism. Service providers in the program may not have an understanding of autism nor be attuned to the specific needs of a student with autism.

If your client's preferred school does not have a program designed specifically for students with autism, then you should encourage them to find a different school. You might suggest that they look for another college nearby that can serve them better.

College students need good high-level organization skills, and you can help your client learn them. For starters, you can work with your client on a checklist of what they need to go to school. You can also help them learn to organize themselves for the school day. You could have them verbally walk through their schedule noting what they need and how long each step will take. You can also role-play their day, looking at scenarios in which they will need to maneuver in order to be independent in the college environment.

Driving & Independence

Being able to drive is the hallmark of independence. Driving can provide an individual a great deal of independence even if they are otherwise dependent on other people. Just being diagnosed with autism does not necessarily mean that an individual cannot get a driver's license, but there are some aspects of autism that can make driving difficult. Driving often requires predicting what the other person is going to do and that can be a problem for someone with autism. Rigid focus on specific topics or activities can also be a problem since driving often requires shifting focus from one important thing to another.

Research on driving and autism is rather limited. One study (Curry et al. 2017) estimated that about 33% (one in three) eligible teenagers with autism (without intellectual disability) obtained their driver's licenses from 1987–1995 compared to 83.5% of teenagers without autism.

That study was based on data that was over 20 years old when the study was published and I have not seen any studies with more recent data. Reimer et al. (2013) conducted a study with a driving simulation program and found that teenagers with autism, on average, did not show any worse driving skills than teenagers without autism.

When it comes to deciding if your client should consider getting his or her license, you really have to look at his or her specific case. Having a discussion with your client and, if possible, family members about the specific challenges your client is likely to face with driving is important. Many states require some sort of physician approval before a person can take their driving test.

Even if your state does not require it, you should ask your client to consider being evaluated by his or her physician to make sure that there are not any limitations that could interfere with safe driving. This could address not only medical issues, but also let the physician express her or his opinion about how your client's autism symptoms might interfere with the physical demands of driving. Having a provisional license (or a "learner's permit" as many states call it) will be an important opportunity for your client to show that he or she can handle all the demands associated with driving.

Keep in mind that the discussion of getting a driver's license is also a very good time to talk about alternatives to driving. Discussing the use of public transportation and ride-sharing services (e.g., Uber, Lyft) can be very helpful for expanding your client's view about how he or she can get around independently even without a driver's license. Addressing the realistic options for riding a bike and/or walking for getting to places your client needs to go is also important.

Given that teenagers in general are waiting longer to get their licenses and are driving less than was the case years ago (Shults, Olsen & Williams, 2015), making use of these alternatives would likely not make him or her different from many of his or her peers.

In Conclusion

In the end, what you want to do is help your teenage and young adult clients be as independent as possible. Even if a client has a considerable amount of functional difficulties it is still going to be the case that they want to be as independent as possible. Throughout this book, the issue of independence has been an important one related to helping teenagers and young adults with autism.

Making use of the information discussed in this chapter will help your clients be as independent with their lives as they possibly can be. If you help you clients reach their maximum level of independence, you will be doing a lot to help them be the best people they can possibly be. And that really is the very essence of what we all try to do as therapists and counselors.

References

For your convenience, purchasers can download and print worksheets and handouts from www.pesi.com/independence

Chapter 1

Anderson, D. K., Maye, M. P., & Lord, C. (2011). Changes in maladaptive behaviors from midchildhood to young adulthood in autism spectrum disorder. *American Journal on Intellectual and Developmental Disabilities, 116(5)*, 381-397.

Biggs, E. E., & Carter, E. W. (2016). Quality of life for transition-age youth with autism or intellectual disability. *Journal of Autism and Developmental Disorders, 46(1)*, 190-204.

Chowdhury, M., Benson, B. A., & Hillier, A. (2010). Changes in restricted repetitive behaviors with age: A study of high-functioning adults with autism spectrum disorders. *Research in Autism Spectrum Disorders, 4(2)*, 210-216.

Groen, W., Teluij, M., Buitelaar, J., & Tendolkar, I. (2010). Amygdala and hippocampus enlargement during adolescence in autism. *Journal of the American Academy of Child & Adolescent Psychiatry, 49(6)*, 552-560.

Keller, R., Basta, R., Salerno, L., & Elia, M. (2017). Autism, epilepsy, and synaptopathies: A not rare association. *Neurological Sciences, 38(8)*, 1353-1361.

Magiati, I., Tay, X. W., & Howlin, P. (2014). Cognitive, language, social and behavioural outcomes in adults with autism spectrum disorders: A systematic review of longitudinal follow-up studies in adulthood. *Clinical Psychology Review, 34(1)*, 73-86.

McGovern, C. W., & Sigman, M. (2005). Continuity and change from early childhood to adolescence in autism. *Journal of Child Psychology and Psychiatry, 46(4)*, 401-408.

O'Hearn, K., Tanaka, J., Lynn, A., Fedor, J., Minshew, N., & Luna, B. (2014). Developmental plateau in visual object processing from adolescence to adulthood in autism. *Brain and Cognition, 90*, 124-134.

Rosenthal, M., Wallace, G. L., Lawson, R., Wills, M. C., Dixon, E., Yerys, B. E., & Kenworthy, L. (2013). Impairments in real-world executive function increase from childhood to adolescence in autism spectrum disorders. *Neuropsychology, 27(1)*, 13.

Smith, L. E., Maenner, M. J., & Seltzer, M. M. (2012). Developmental trajectories in adolescents and adults with autism: The case of daily living skills. *Journal of the American Academy of Child & Adolescent Psychiatry, 51(6)*, 622-631.

Taheri, A., Perry, A., & Minnes, P. (2016). Examining the social participation of children and adolescents with intellectual disabilities and autism spectrum disorder in relation to peers. *Journal of Intellectual Disability Research, 60(5)*, 435-443.

Walton, K. M., & Ingersoll, B. R. (2013). Improving social skills in adolescents and adults with autism and severe to profound intellectual disability: A review of the literature. *Journal of Autism and Developmental Disorders, 43(3)*, 594-615.

Yitzchak Frank, M. D., Jamison, J. M., Tavassoli, T., & Kolevzon, M. D. (2017). A Prospective study of neurological abnormalities in Phelan-McDermid syndrome. *Journal of Rare Disorders, 5(1)*, 1-13.

Chapter 2

American Psychiatric Association. (2013). Diagnostic and statistical manual of mental disorders, fifth edition (*DSM-5*). Washington, DC: American Psychiatric Publications.

Baron-Cohen, S., Hoekstra, R. A., Knickmeyer, R. & Wheelwright, S. (2006). The autism spectrum quotient (AQ) – adolescent version. *Journal of Autism & Developmental Disorders, 36(3)*, 343-350.

Baron-Cohen, S., Wheelwright, S., Skinner, R., Martin, J., & Clubley, E. (2001). The autism-spectrum quotient (AQ): Evidence from Asperger syndrome/high-functioning autism, males and females, scientists and mathematicians. *Journal of Autism and Developmental Disorders, 31(1)*, 5-17.

Beck, A. T., & Steer, R. A. (1990). Manual for the Beck anxiety inventory. San Antonio, TX: Psychological Corporation.

Beck, A. T., Steer, R. A., & Brown, G. K. (1996). Beck depression inventory-II. Psychological Corporation: San Antonio, TX.

Beaudet, A. L. (2017). Brain carnitine deficiency causes nonsyndromic autism with an extreme male bias: A hypothesis. *BioEssays, 39*(8), 1700012.

Brown, T. E. (2009). ADD/ADHD and impaired executive function in clinical practice. *Current Attention Disorders Reports, 1*(1), 37-41.

Brown, C., & Dunn, W. (2002). Adult/adolescent sensory profile: User's manual. San Antonio, TX: Psychological Corporation.

Garofoli, F., Lombardi, G., Orcesi, S., Pisoni, C., Mazzucchelli, I., Angelini, M., Balottin, U., & Stronati, M. (2017). An Italian prospective experience on the association between congenital cytomegalovirus infection and autistic spectrum disorder. *Journal of Autism and Developmental Disorders, 47*(5), 1490-1495.

Hamill, D. D., Brown, V. L., Larsen, S. C., & Wiederholt, J. L. (2016). *Test of adolescent and adult language-fourth edition.* Pearson Assessment.

Huerta, M., & Lord, C. (2012). Diagnostic evaluation of autism spectrum disorders. *Pediatric Clinics of North America, 59*(1), 103-111.

Lord, C., Rutter, M., DiLavore, P., Risi, S., Gotham, K., & Bishop, S. (2012). Autism diagnostic observation schedule–second edition (ADOS-2). Los Angeles, CA: Western Psychological Corporation.

Manohar, H., Kuppili, P. P., Kandasamy, P., Chandrasekaran, V., & Rajkumar, R. P. (2018). Implications of comorbid ADHD in ASD interventions and outcome: Results from a naturalistic follow-up study from south India. *Asian Journal of Psychiatry, 33*, 68-73.

Ozonoff, S., Goodlin-Jones, B. L., & Solomon, M. (2005). Evidence-based assessment of autism spectrum disorders in children and adolescents. *Journal of Clinical Child and Adolescent Psychology, 34*(3), 523-540.

Roth, R. M., & Gioia, G. A. (2005). Behavior rating inventory of executive function—adult version. Lutz, FL: Psychological Assessment Resources.

Russell, A. J., Murphy, C. M., Wilson, E., Gillan, N., Brown, C., Robertson, D. M., & McAlonan, G. M. (2016). The mental health of individuals referred for assessment of autism spectrum disorder in adulthood: A clinic report. *Autism, 20*(5), 623-627.

Rutter, M., Bailey, A., & Lord, C. (2003). The social communication questionnaire: Manual. Western Psychological Services.

Rutter, M., Le Couteur, A., & Lord, C. (2003). Autism diagnostic interview-revised. Los Angeles, CA: Western Psychological Services.

Sappok, T., Gaul, I., Bergmann, T., Dziobek, I., Bölte, S., Diefenbacher, A., & Heinrich, M. (2014). The diagnostic behavioral assessment for autism spectrum disorder—revised: A screening instrument for adults with intellectual disability suspected of autism spectrum disorders. *Research in Autism Spectrum Disorders, 8*(4), 362-375.

Schaaf, R. C., & Lane, A. E. (2015). Toward a best-practice protocol for assessment of sensory features in ASD. *Journal of Autism and Developmental Disorders, 45*(5), 1380-1395.

Thorndike, R. L., Hagen, E. P., & Sattler, J. M. (1986). Stanford-Binet intelligence scale. Riverside Publishing Company.

Wechsler, D. (2008). Wechsler adult intelligence scale–fourth edition (WAIS–IV). San Antonio, TX: NCS Pearson.

White, S. W., Smith, L. A., & Schry, A. R. (2014). Assessment of global functioning in adolescents with autism spectrum disorders: Utility of the developmental disability–child global assessment scale. *Autism, 18*(4), 362-369.

Chapter 3

Baker, M. J., Koegel, R. L., & Koegel, L. K. (1998). Increasing the social behavior of young children with autism using their obsessive behaviors. *Journal of the Association for Persons with Severe Handicaps, 23*(4), 300-308.

Bolton Oetzel, K., & Scherer, D. G. (2003). Therapeutic engagement with adolescents in psychotherapy. *Psychotherapy: Theory, Research, Practice, Training, 40*(3), 215.

Charlop, M. H., Kurtz, P. F., & Casey, F. G. (1990). Using aberrant behaviors as reinforcers for autistic children. *Journal of Applied Behavior Analysis, 23*(2), 163-181.

Cottenceau, H., Roux, S., Blanc, R., Lenoir, P., Bonnet-Brilhault, F., & Barthélémy, C. (2012). Quality of life of adolescents with autism spectrum disorders: Comparison to adolescents with diabetes. *European Child & Adolescent Psychiatry, 21*(5), 289-296.

Drummond, K. D. (2013). *Self-concept, behavioural attributions and self-awareness in adolescents with autism spectrum disorder: A mixed-methods approach* (Doctoral dissertation, University of Toronto (Canada)).

Egilson, S. T., Ólafsdóttir, L. B., Leósdóttir, T., & Saemundsen, E. (2017). Quality of life of high-functioning children and youth with autism spectrum disorder and typically developing peers: Self and proxy-reports. *Autism, 21*(2), 133-141.

Elfers, T. (2015). *Identity formation and well-being in youth with and without autism spectrum disorder* (Doctoral dissertation, Arts & Social Sciences: Department of Psychology).

Hurlbutt, K., & Chalmers, L. (2002). Adults with autism speak out: Perceptions of their life experiences. *Focus on Autism and Other Developmental Disabilities, 17*(2), 103-111.

Jackson, P., Skirrow, P., & Hare, D. J. (2012). Asperger through the looking glass: An exploratory study of self-understanding in people with Asperger's syndrome. *Journal of Autism and Developmental Disorders, 42*(5), 697-706.

Leach, M. J. (2005). Rapport: A key to treatment success. *Complementary Therapies in Clinical Practice, 11*(4), 262-265.

Martin, N. (2008). Assessing portrait drawings created by children and adolescents with autism spectrum disorder. *Art Therapy, 25*(1), 15-23.

Mogensen, L., & Mason, J. (2015). The meaning of a label for teenagers negotiating identity: Experiences with autism spectrum disorder. *Sociology of Health & Illness, 37*(2), 255-269.

Mulligan, S., White, B. P., & Arthanat, S. (2014). An examination of occupation-based, client-centered, evidence-based occupational therapy practices in New Hampshire. *OTJR: Occupation, Participation and Health, 34*(2), 106-116.

Norfolk, T., Birdi, K., & Walsh, D. (2007). The role of empathy in establishing rapport in the consultation: A new model. *Medical Education, 41*(7), 690-697.

Pfeifer, J. H., Merchant, J. S., Colich, N. L., Hernandez, L. M., Rudie, J. D., & Dapretto, M. (2013). Neural and behavioral responses during self-evaluative processes differ in youth with and without autism. *Journal of Autism and Developmental Disorders*, 1-14.

Puleo, C. M., & Kendall, P. C. (2011). Anxiety disorders in typically developing youth: Autism spectrum symptoms as a predictor of cognitive-behavioral treatment. *Journal of Autism and Developmental Disorders, 41*(3), 275-286.

Reaven, J., Blakeley-Smith, A., Leuthe, E., Moody, E., & Hepburn, S. (2012). Facing your fears in adolescence: Cognitive-behavioral therapy for high-functioning autism spectrum disorders and anxiety. *Autism Research and Treatment, 2012.*

Richards, M. (2016). 'You've got autism because you like order and you do not look into my eyes': Some reflections on understanding the label of 'autism spectrum disorder' from a dishuman perspective. *Disability & Society, 31*(9), 1301-1305.

Vismara, L. A., & Lyons, G. L. (2007). Using perseverative interests to elicit joint attention behaviors in young children with autism: Theoretical and clinical implications for understanding motivation. *Journal of Positive Behavior Interventions, 9*(4), 214-228.

Chapter 4

Brooks, S., & Paterson, G. (2011). Using contact work in interactions with adults with learning disabilities and autistic spectrum disorders. *British Journal of Learning Disabilities, 39*(2), 161-166.

Carrick, L., & McKenzie, S. (2011). A heuristic examination of the application of pre-therapy skills and the person-centered approach in the field of autism. *Person-Centered & Experiential Psychotherapies, 10*(2), 73-88.

Emanuel, C. (2015). An accidental Pokemon expert: Contemporary psychoanalysis on the autism spectrum. *International Journal of Psychoanalytic Self Psychology, 10*(1), 53-68.

Field, T., Field, T., Sanders, C., & Nadel, J. (2001). Children with autism display more social behaviors after repeated imitation sessions. *Autism, 5(3)*, 317-323.

Hagner, D., Kurtz, A., May, J., & Cloutier, H. (2014). Person-centered planning for transition-aged youth with autism spectrum disorders. *Journal of Rehabilitation, 80(1)*, 4.

Hobson, R. P. (2011). On the relations between autism and psychoanalytic thought and practice. *Psychoanalytic Psychotherapy, 25(3)*, 229-244.

Koenig, K., & Levine, M. (2011). Psychotherapy for individuals with autism spectrum disorders. *Journal of Contemporary Psychotherapy, 41(1)*, 29-36.

Pfeifer, J. H., Merchant, J. S., Colich, N. L., Hernandez, L. M., Rudie, J. D., & Dapretto, M. (2013). Neural and behavioral responses during self-evaluative processes differ in youth with and without autism. *Journal of Autism and Developmental Disorders*, 1-14.

Prouty, G. (2003). Pre-therapy: A newer development in the psychotherapy of schizophrenia. *Journal of the American Academy of Psychoanalysis and Dynamic Psychiatry, 31(1: Special issue)*, 59-73.

Rogers, C. (1957). The necessary and sufficient conditions of therapeutic personality change. *Journal of Consulting Psychology, 21(2)*, 95-103.

Shuttleworth, J. (1999). The suffering of Asperger children and the challenge they present to psychoanalytic thinking. *Journal of Child Psychotherapy, 25(2)*, 239-265.

Singletary, W. M. (2015). An integrative model of autism spectrum disorder: ASD as a neurobiological disorder of experienced environmental deprivation, early life stress and allostatic overload. *Neuropsychoanalysis, 17(2)*, 81-119.

Tantam, D. (2000). Psychological disorder in adolescents and adults with Asperger syndrome. *Autism, 4(1)*, 47-62.

Volkmar, F. R. (2011). Asperger's disorder: Implications for psychoanalysis. *Psychoanalytic Inquiry, 31(3)*, 334-344.

Chapter 5

Epstein, R. M., Siegel, D. J., & Silberman, J. (2008). Self-monitoring in clinical practice: A challenge for medical educators. *Journal of Continuing Education in the Health Professions, 28*(1), 5-13.

Grynszpan, O., Nadel, J., Martin, J. C., Simonin, J., Bailleul, P., Wang, Y., & Constant, J. (2012). Self-monitoring of gaze in high functioning autism. *Journal of Autism and Developmental Disorders, 42*(8), 1642-1650.

Hume, K., Loftin, R., & Lantz, J. (2009). Increasing independence in autism spectrum disorders: A review of three focused interventions. *Journal of Autism and Developmental Disorders, 39*(9), 1329-1338.

Kohlenberg, R. J., & Tsai, M. (1994). Functional analytic psychotherapy: A radical behavioral approach to treatment and integration. *Journal of Psychotherapy Integration, 4*(3), 175.

Landes, S. J., Kanter, J. W., Weeks, C. E., & Busch, A. M. (2013). The impact of the active components of functional analytic psychotherapy on idiographic target behaviors. *Journal of Contextual Behavioral Science, 2*(1), 49-57.

Tiger, J. H., Fisher, W. W., & Bouxsein, K. J. (2009). Therapist- and self-monitored DRO contingencies as a treatment for the self-injurious skin picking of a young man with Asperger syndrome. *Journal of Applied Behavior Analysis, 42*(2), 315-319.

Tsai, M., Callaghan, G. M., & Kohlenberg, R. J. (2013). The use of awareness, courage, therapeutic love, and behavioral interpretation in functional analytic psychotherapy. *Psychotherapy, 50*(3), 366.

Chapter 6

Barnhill, G. P., Tapscott Cook, K., Tebbenkamp, K., & Smith Myles, B. (2002). The effectiveness of social skills intervention targeting nonverbal communication for adolescents with Asperger syndrome and related pervasive developmental delays. *Focus on Autism and Other Developmental Disabilities, 17*(2), 112-118.

Bölte, S., Hubl, D., Feineis-Matthews, S., Prvulovic, D., Dierks, T., & Poustka, F. (2006). Facial affect recognition training in autism: Can we animate the fusiform gyrus? *Behavioral Neuroscience, 120*(1), 211.

Gresham, F. M., Sugai, G., & Horner, R. H. (2001). Interpreting outcomes of social skills training for students with high-incidence disabilities. *Exceptional Children, 67*(3), 331-344.

Grynszpan, O., Nadel, J., Martin, J. C., Simonin, J., Bailleul, P., Wang, Y., Gepner, D., LeBarillier, F., & Constant, J. (2012). Self-monitoring of gaze in high functioning autism. *Journal of Autism and Developmental Disorders, 42*(8), 1642-1650.

Helt, M., Kelley, E., Kinsbourne, M., Pandey, J., Boorstein, H., Herbert, M., & Fein, D. (2008). Can children with autism recover? If so, how? *Neuropsychology Review, 18*(4), 339-366.

Kandalaft, M. R., Didehbani, N., Krawczyk, D. C., Allen, T. T., & Chapman, S. B. (2013). Virtual reality social cognition training for young adults with high-functioning autism. *Journal of Autism and Developmental Disorders*, 1-11.

Kars, J. S., Van Hecke, A. V., Carson, A. M., Stevens, S., Schohl, K., & Dolan, B. (2015). Parent and family outcomes of PEERS: A social skills intervention for adolescents with autism spectrum disorder. *Journal of Autism and Developmental Disorders, 45*(3), 752-765.

Koegel, L. K., Koegel, R. L., Miller, A. R., & Detar, W. J. (2014). Issues and interventions for autism spectrum disorders during adolescence and beyond. *Handbook of Autism and Pervasive Developmental Disorders, Fourth Edition*.

Jobe, L. E., & White, S. W. (2007). Loneliness, social relationships, and a broader autism phenotype in college students. *Personality and Individual Differences, 42*(8), 1479-1489.

Laugeson, E. A., Frankel, F., Mogil, C., & Dillon, A. R. (2009). Parent-assisted social skills training to improve friendships in teens with autism spectrum disorders. *Journal of Autism and Developmental Disorders, 39*(4), 596-606.

Laugeson, E. A., Frankel, F., Gantman, A., Dillon, A. R., & Mogil, C. (2012). Evidence-based social skills training for adolescents with autism spectrum disorders: The UCLA PEERS program. *Journal of Autism and Developmental Disorders, 42*(6), 1025-1036.

Laugeson, E. A., Ellingsen, R., Sanderson, J., Tucci, L., & Bates, S. (2014). The ABC's of teaching social skills to adolescents with autism spectrum disorder in the classroom: The UCLA PEERS® program. *Journal of Autism and Developmental Disorders, 44*(9), 2244-2256.

Linden Labs (2003). Second Life (version 2.1) [Software]. Available from http://secondlife.com/

Mesibov, G. B. (1984). Social skills training with verbal autistic adolescents and adults: A program model. *Journal of Autism and Developmental Disorders, 14*(4), 395-404.

Parsons, S., & Mitchell, P. (2002). The potential of virtual reality in social skills training for people with autistic spectrum disorders. *Journal of Intellectual Disability Research, 46*(5), 430-443.

Ramdoss, S., Machalicek, W., Rispoli, M., Mulloy, A., Lang, R., & O'Reilly, M. (2012). Computer-based interventions to improve social and emotional skills in individuals with autism spectrum disorders: A systematic review. *Developmental Neurorehabilitation, 15*(2), 119-135.

Reichow, B., & Volkmar, F. R. (2010). Social skills interventions for individuals with autism: Evaluation for evidence-based practices within a best evidence synthesis framework. *Journal of Autism and Developmental Disorders, 40*(2), 149-166.

Silver, M., & Oakes, P. (2001). Evaluation of a new computer intervention to teach people with autism or Asperger syndrome to recognize and predict emotions in others. *Autism, 5*(3), 299-316.

Chapter 7

Achenbach, T. M., & Rescorla, L. A. (2003). University of Vermont, Research Center for Children, Youth, & Families; Burlington, VT. *Manual for the ASEBA Adult Forms & Profiles*.

Anderson, S., & Morris, J. (2006). Cognitive behaviour therapy for people with Asperger syndrome. *Behavioural and Cognitive Psychotherapy, 34*(3), 293-303.

Beck, A. T., Steer, R. A., & Brown, G. K. (1996). Manual for the Beck Depression Inventory. San Antonio, TX: The Psychological Corporation.

Bertilsdotter Rosqvist, H., Brownlow, C., & O'Dell, L. (2015). "What's the point of having friends?": Reformulating notions of the meaning of friends and friendship among autistic people. *Disability Studies Quarterly (DSQ), 35*(4).

Best, P., Manktelow, R., & Taylor, B. (2014). Online communication, social media and adolescent wellbeing: A systematic narrative review. *Children and Youth Services Review*, 41, 27-36.

Best, P., Taylor, B., & Manktelow, R. (2015). I've 500 friends, but who are my mates? Investigating the influence of online friend networks on adolescent wellbeing. *Journal of Public Mental Health, 14*(3), 135-148.

Burenk, A. P., Dijkstra, P., & Roberts, S. C. (2012). The social animal within organizations. *Applied Evolutionary Psychology*, 36.

Cacioppo, J. T., & Hawkley, L. C. (2009). Perceived social isolation and cognition. *Trends in Cognitive Sciences, 13*(10), 447-454.

Demir, M., & Davidson, I. (2013). Toward a better understanding of the relationship between friendship and happiness: Perceived responses to capitalization attempts, feelings of mattering, and satisfaction of basic psychological needs in same-sex best friendships as predictors of happiness. *Journal of Happiness Studies, 14*(2), 525-550.

Detillion, C. E., Craft, T. K., Glasper, E. R., Prendergast, B. J., & DeVries, A. C. (2004). Social facilitation of wound healing. *Psychoneuroendocrinology, 29*(8), 1004-1011.

Foggo, R. S. V., & Webster, A. A. (2017). Understanding the social experiences of adolescent females on the autism spectrum. *Research in Autism Spectrum Disorders*, 35, 74-85.

Gillespie, B. J., Lever, J., Frederick, D., & Royce, T. (2015). Close adult friendships, gender, and the life cycle. *Journal of Social and Personal Relationships*, 32(6), 709-736.

Gotham, K., Unruh, K., & Lord, C. (2015). Depression and its measurement in verbal adolescents and adults with autism spectrum disorder. *Autism*, 19(4), 491-504.

Hennessy, M. B. (1984). Presence of companion moderates arousal of monkeys with restricted social experience. *Physiology & Behavior*, 33(5), 693-698.

Jamil, R., Gragg, M. N., & DePape, A. M. (2017). The broad autism phenotype: Implications for empathy and friendships in emerging adults. *Personality and Individual Differences*, 111, 199-204.

Marston, D., & Maple, T. (2016). *Comparative Psychology for Clinical Psychologists and Therapists*. London: Jessica Kingsley Publishers.

Matthews, T., Danese, A., Wertz, J., Odgers, C. L., Ambler, A., Moffitt, T. E., & Arseneault, L. (2016). Social isolation, loneliness and depression in young adulthood: A behavioural genetic analysis. *Social Psychiatry and Psychiatric Epidemiology*, 51(3), 339-348.

Nabors, L., Hawkins, R., Yockey, A. R., Booker, S., & Tipkemper, A. (2017). Adolescents with autism spectrum disorder: Friendships and social interactions. *Advances in Neurodevelopmental Disorders*, 1(1), 14-20.

Peñagarikano, O., Lázaro, M. T., Lu, X. H., Gordon, A., Dong, H., Lam, H. A., Petes, E., Maidment, N., Murphy, N., Yang, X., Golshani, P., & Geschwind, D. H. (2015). Exogenous and evoked oxytocin restores social behavior in the Cntnap2 mouse model of autism. *Science Translational Medicine*, 7(271), 271ra8-271ra8.

Reis, H. T., & Collins, W. A. (2004). Relationships, human behavior and psychological science. *Current Directions in Psychological Science*, 13(6), 233-237.

Reynolds, W. M., & Baker, J. (1988) Assessment of depression in persons with mental retardation. *American Journal on Mental Retardation*, 93(1), 93–105.

Spithoven, A. W., Lodder, G. M., Goossens, L., Bijttebier, P., Bastin, M., Verhagen, M., & Scholte, R. H. (2017). Adolescents' loneliness and depression associated with friendship experiences and well-being: A person-centered approach. *Journal of Youth and Adolescence*, 46(2), 429-441.

Stavropoulos, K. M., & Carver, L. J. (2013). Research review: Social motivation and oxytocin in autism–implications for joint attention development and intervention. *Journal of Child Psychology and Psychiatry* 54(6), 603-618.

Vogt, J. L., Coe, C. L., & Levine, S. (1981). Behavioral and adrenocorticoid responsiveness of squirrel monkeys to a live snake: Is flight necessarily stressful? *Behavioral and Neural Biology*, 32(4), 391-405.

Wainer, A. L., Block, N., Donnellan, M. B., & Ingersoll, B. (2013). The broader autism phenotype and friendships in non-clinical dyads. *Journal of Autism and Developmental Disorders*, 43(10), 2418-2425.

Young, L. J., & Wang, Z. (2004). The neurobiology of pair bonding. *Nature Neuroscience*, 7(10), 1048-1054.

Chapter 8

Anckarsäter, H. (2006). Central nervous changes in social dysfunction: Autism, aggression, and psychopathy. *Brain Research Bulletin*, 69(3), 259-265.

Bird, G., Silani, G., Brindley, R., White, S., Frith, U., & Singer, T. (2010). Empathic brain responses in insula are modulated by levels of alexithymia but not autism. *Brain*, 133(5), 1515-1525.

Blair, R. J. R. (2008). Fine cuts of empathy and the amygdala: Dissociable deficits in psychopathy and autism. *The Quarterly Journal of Experimental Psychology*, 61(1), 157-170.

Blakemore, S. J. (2010). The developing social brain: Implications for education. *Neuron*, 65(6), 744-747.

Brosnan, J., & Healy, O. (2011). A review of behavioral interventions for the treatment of aggression in individuals with developmental disabilities. *Research in Developmental Disabilities*, 32(2), 437-446.

Fitzgerald, M. (2015). Autism and school shootings—Overlap of autism (Asperger syndrome) and general psychopathy. In *Autism Spectrum Disorder-Recent Advances*. InTech.

Koslowski, N., Klein, K., Arnold, K., Kösters, M., Schützwohl, M., Salize, H. J., & Puschner, B. (2016). Effectiveness of interventions for adults with mild to moderate intellectual disabilities and mental health problems: Systematic review and meta-analysis. *The British Journal of Psychiatry*, 209(6), 469-474.

Mazurek, M. O., Kanne, S. M., & Wodka, E. L. (2013). Physical aggression in children and adolescents with autism spectrum disorders. *Research in Autism Spectrum Disorders, 7*(3), 455-465.

Patel, S., Day, T. N., Jones, N., & Mazefsky, C. A. (2017). Association between anger rumination and autism symptom severity, depression symptoms, aggression, and general dysregulation in adolescents with autism spectrum disorder. *Autism*, *21(2)*, 181-189.

Raine, A. (2002). Biosocial studies of antisocial and violent behavior in children and adults: A review. *Journal of Abnormal Child Psychology*, *30*(4), 311-326.

Samson, A. C., Hardan, A. Y., Podell, R. W., Phillips, J. M., & Gross, J. J. (2015). Emotion regulation in children and adolescents with autism spectrum disorder. *Autism Research*, *8*(1), 9-18.

Singh, N. N., Lancioni, G. E., Manikam, R., Winton, A. S., Singh, A. N., Singh, J., & Singh, A. D. (2011). A mindfulness-based strategy for self-management of aggressive behavior in adolescents with autism. *Research in Autism Spectrum Disorders*, *5*(3), 1153-1158.

Smith, A. (2009). The empathy imbalance hypothesis of autism: A theoretical approach to cognitive and emotional empathy in autistic development. *The Psychological Record*, *59*(2), 273.

Sofronoff, K., Attwood, T., Hinton, S., & Levin, I. (2007). A randomized controlled trial of a cognitive behavioural intervention for anger management in children diagnosed with Asperger syndrome. *Journal of Autism and Developmental Disorders*, *37*(7), 1203-1214.

Sukhodolsky, D. G., Smith, S. D., McCauley, S. A., Ibrahim, K., & Piasecka, J. B. (2016). Behavioral interventions for anger, irritability, and aggression in children and adolescents. *Journal of Child and Adolescent Psychopharmacology*, *26*(1), 58-64.

Wallace, G. L., Shaw, P., Lee, N. R., Clasen, L. S., Raznahan, A., Lenroot, R. K., Martin, A., & Giedd, J. N. (2012). Distinct cortical correlates of autistic versus antisocial traits in a longitudinal sample of typically developing youth. *Journal of Neuroscience*, *32*(14), 4856-4860.

Chapter 9

Attwood, T. (1997). *Asperger's syndrome: A guide for parents and professionals.* London: Jessica Kingsley Publishers.

Baker, M. J., Koegel, R. L., & Koegel, L. K. (1998). Increasing the social behavior of young children with autism using their obsessive behaviors. *Journal of the Association for Persons with Severe Handicaps*, *23*(4), 300-308.

Berkson, G. (1983). Repetitive stereotyped behaviors. *American Journal of Mental Deficiency*, *88*, 239-246.

Boyd, B. A., McDonough, S. G., & Bodfish, J. W. (2012). Evidence-based behavioral interventions for repetitive behaviors in autism. *Journal of Autism and Developmental Disorders*, *42*(6), 1236-1248.

Cassella, M., Sidener, T., & Progar, R. (2011). Response interruption and redirection for stereotypy in children with autism. *Journal of Applied Behavior Analysis*, *44(1)*, 169-173.

Charlop-Christy, M. H., & Haymes, L. K. (1996). Using obsessions as reinforcers with and without mild reductive procedures to decrease inappropriate behaviors of children with autism. *Journal of Autism and Developmental Disorders*, *26*(5), 527-546.

Fisher, W. W., Rodriguez, N. M., & Owen, T. M. (2013). Functional assessment and treatment of perseverative speech about restricted topics in an adolescent with Asperger syndrome. *Journal of Applied Behavior Analysis*, *46*(1), 307-311.

Hung, D. W. (1978). Using self-stimulation as reinforcement for autistic children. *Journal of Autism and Developmental Disorders*, *8*(3), 355-366.

Ivy, J. W., & Schreck, K. A. (2016). The efficacy of ABA for individuals with autism across the lifespan. *Current Developmental Disorders Reports*, *3*(1), 57-66.

Joyce, C., Honey, E., Leekam, S. R., Barrett, S. L., & Rodgers, J. (2017). Anxiety, intolerance of uncertainty and restricted and repetitive behaviour: Insights directly from young people with ASD. *Journal of Autism and Developmental Disorders*, *47*(12), 3789-3802.

Kern, L., Koegel, R. L., & Dunlap, G. (1984). The influence of vigorous versus mild exercise on autistic stereotyped behaviors. *Journal of Autism and Developmental Disorders*, *14*(1), 57-67.

Koegel, R. L., Fredeen, R., Kim, S., Danial, J., Rubinstein, D., & Koegel, L. (2012). Using perseverative interests to improve interactions between adolescents with autism and their typical peers in school settings. *Journal of Positive Behavior Interventions*, *14*(3), 133-141.

Lang, R., Mahoney, R., El Zein, F., Delaune, E., & Amidon, M. (2011). Evidence to practice: Treatment of anxiety in individuals with autism spectrum disorders. *Neuropsychiatric Disease and Treatment*, *7*, 27.

Lovaas, I., Newsom, C., & Hickman, C. (1987). Self-stimulatory behavior and perceptual reinforcement. *Journal of Applied Behavior Analysis, 20*, 45-68.

Patel, S., Day, T. N., Jones, N., & Mazefsky, C. A. (2017). Association between anger rumination and autism symptom severity, depression symptoms, aggression, and general dysregulation in adolescents with autism spectrum disorder. *Autism, 21*(2), 181-189.

Rehfeldt, R. A., & Chambers, M. R. (2003). Functional analysis and treatment of verbal perseverations displayed by an adult with autism. *Journal of Applied Behavior Analysis, 36*(2), 259-261.

Roth, M. E., Gillis, J. M., & Reed, F. D. D. (2014). A meta-analysis of behavioral interventions for adolescents and adults with autism spectrum disorders. *Journal of Behavioral Education, 23*(2), 258-286.

Salisbury, J. M. (2016). Reduction of Stereotypy in Adolescents with Autism Using Visual and Auditory Cues. *Action Thesis Submitted in Partial Fulfillment of the Requirements for the Degree of Master of Arts in Education California State University, Monterey Bay, May 2016.*

Spek, A. A., van Ham N.C., Nyklíček, I. (2013). Mindfulness-based therapy in adults with an autism spectrum disorder: A randomized controlled trial. *Research in Developmental Disabilities. 34*(1), 246–253.

Wilder, D. A., Masuda, A., O'Connor, C., & Baham, M. (2001). Brief functional analysis and treatment of bizarre vocalizations in an adult with schizophrenia. *Journal of Applied Behavior Analysis, 34*(1), 65-68.

Williams, D. L., Siegel, M., & Mazefsky, C. A. (2017). Problem behaviors in autism spectrum disorder: Association with verbal ability and adapting/coping skills. *Journal of Autism and Developmental Disorders*, 1-10.

Wolery, M., Kirk, K., & Gast, D. L. (1985). Stereotypic behavior as a reinforcer: Effects and side effects. *Journal of Autism and Developmental Disorders, 15*(2), 149-161.

Chapter 10

Burke, M., & Heller, T. (2016). Individual, parent and social–environmental correlates of caregiving experiences among parents of adults with autism spectrum disorder. *Journal of Intellectual Disability Research, 60*(5), 401-411.

Chamak, B., & Bonniau, B. (2016). Trajectories, long-term outcomes and family experiences of 76 adults with autism spectrum disorder. *Journal of Autism and Developmental Disorders, 46*(3), 1084-1095.

Krauss, M. W., Seltzer, M. M., & Jacobson, H. T. (2005). Adults with autism living at home or in non-family settings: Positive and negative aspects of residential status. *Journal of Intellectual Disability Research, 49*(2), 111-124.

Mazefsky, C. A., Folstein, S. E., & Lainhart, J. E. (2008). Overrepresentation of mood and anxiety disorders in adults with autism and their first-degree relatives: What does it mean? *Autism Research, 1*(3), 193-197.

Seltzer, M. M., Krauss, M. W., Orsmond, G. I., & Vestal, C. (2000). Families of adolescents and adults with autism: Uncharted territory. *International Review of Research in Mental Retardation, 23*, 267-294.

Seltzer, M. M., Shattuck, P., Abbeduto, L., & Greenberg, J. S. (2004). Trajectory of development in adolescents and adults with autism. *Developmental Disabilities Research Reviews, 10*(4), 234-247.

Taylor, J. L., & Mailick, M. R. (2014). A longitudinal examination of 10-year change in vocational and educational activities for adults with autism spectrum disorders. *Developmental Psychology, 50*(3), 699.

Taylor, J. L., & Seltzer, M. M. (2011). Employment and post-secondary educational activities for young adults with autism spectrum disorders during the transition to adulthood. *Journal of Autism and Developmental Disorders, 41*(5), 566-574.

Weiss, J. A., Tint, A., Paquette-Smith, M., & Lunsky, Y. (2016). Perceived self-efficacy in parents of adolescents and adults with autism spectrum disorder. *Autism, 20*(4), 425-434.

Chapter 11

Dauphin, M., Kinney, E. M., Stromer, R., & Koegel, R. L. (2004). Using video-enhanced activity schedules and matrix training to teach sociodramatic play to a child with autism. *Journal of Positive Behavior Interventions, 6*(4), 238-250.

De Marchena, A. B., Eigsti, I. M., & Yerys, B. E. (2015). Brief report: Generalization weaknesses in verbally fluent children and adolescents with autism spectrum disorder. *Journal of Autism and Developmental Disorders, 45*(10), 3370-3376.

Froehlich, A. L., Anderson, J. S., Bigler, E. D., Miller, J. S., Lange, N. T., DuBray, M. B., & Lainhart, J. E. (2012). Intact prototype formation but impaired generalization in autism. *Research in Autism Spectrum Disorders, 6*(2), 921-930.

Kelly, W. J., Salzberg, C. L., Levy, S. M., Warrenteltz, R. B., Adams, T. W., Crouse, T. R., & Beegle, G. P. (1983). The effects of role-playing and self-monitoring on the generalization of vocational social skills by behaviorally disordered adolescents. *Behavioral Disorders*, 27-35.

Lasater, M. W., & Brady, M. P. (1995). Effects of video self-modeling and feedback on task fluency: A home-based intervention. *Education and Treatment of Children*, 389-407.

Mechling, L. C., & Ortega-Hurndon, F. (2007). Computer-based video instruction to teach young adults with moderate intellectual disabilities to perform multiple step, job tasks in a generalized setting. *Education and Training in Developmental Disabilities*, 24-37.

Neely, L. C., Ganz, J. B., Davis, J. L., Boles, M. B., Hong, E. R., Ninci, J., & Gilliland, W. D. (2016). Generalization and maintenance of functional living skills for individuals with autism spectrum disorder: A review and meta-analysis. *Review Journal of Autism and Developmental Disorders*, *3*(1), 37-47.

Rosenberg, N., Congdon, M., Schwartz, I., & Kamps, D. (2015). Use of say-do correspondence training to increase generalization of social interaction skills at recess for children with autism spectrum disorder. *Education and Training in Autism and Developmental Disabilities*, *50*(2), 213.

Smith, K. A., Ayres, K. A., Alexander, J., Ledford, J. R., Shepley, C., & Shepley, S. B. (2016). Initiation and generalization of self-instructional skills in adolescents with autism and intellectual disability. *Journal of Autism and Developmental Disorders*, *46*(4), 1196-1209.

Wert, B. Y., & Neisworth, J. T. (2003). Effects of video self-modeling on spontaneous requesting in children with autism. *Journal of Positive Behavior Interventions*, *5*(1), 30-34.

Chapter 12

Curry, A. E., Yerys, B. E., Huang, P., & Metzger, K. B. (2017). Longitudinal study of driver licensing rates among adolescents and young adults with autism spectrum disorder. *Autism, 22(4), 479-488.*

Gerhardt, P. F., & Lainer, I. (2011). Addressing the needs of adolescents and adults with autism: A crisis on the horizon. *Journal of Contemporary Psychotherapy*, *41*(1), 37-45.

Hendricks, D. R., & Wehman, P. (2009). Transition from school to adulthood for youth with autism spectrum disorders: Review and recommendations. *Focus on Autism and Other Developmental Disabilities*, *24*(2), 77-88.

Henninger, N. A., & Taylor, J. L. (2013). Outcomes in adults with autism spectrum disorders: A historical perspective. *Autism*, *17*(1), 103-116.

Howlin, P., Alcock, J., & Burkin, C. (2005). An 8 year follow-up of a specialist supported employment service for high-ability adults with autism or Asperger syndrome. *Autism*, *9*(5), 533-549.

Matson, J. L., Rivet, T. T., Fodstad, J. C., Dempsey, T., & Boisjoli, J. A. (2009). Examination of adaptive behavior differences in adults with autism spectrum disorders and intellectual disability. *Research in Developmental Disabilities*, *30*(6), 1317-1325.

Reimer, B., Fried, R., Mehler, B., Joshi, G., Bolfek, A., Godfrey, K. M., & Biederman, J. (2013). Brief report: Examining driving behavior in young adults with high functioning autism spectrum disorders: A pilot study using a driving simulation paradigm. *Journal of Autism and Developmental Disorders*, *43*(9), 2211-2217.

Shults, R. A., Olsen, E., & Williams, A. F. (2015). Driving among high school students-United States, 2013. *MMWR. Morbidity and Mortality Weekly Report*, *64*(12), 313-317.

Smith, L. E., Maenner, M. J., & Seltzer, M. M. (2012). Developmental trajectories in adolescents and adults with autism: The case of daily living skills. *Journal of the American Academy of Child & Adolescent Psychiatry*, *51*(6), 622-631.

10/19